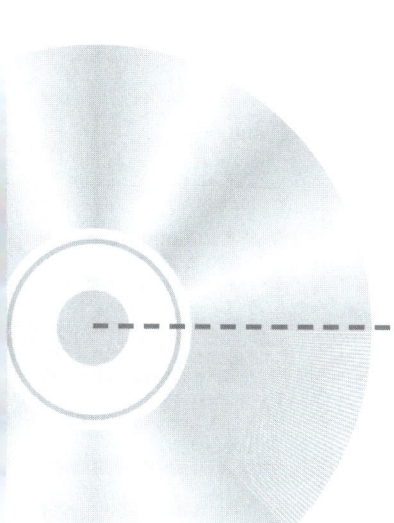

The Elementary Teacher's Digital Toolbox

Helen Hoffner
Holy Family University

PEARSON
Merrill Prentice Hall

Upper Saddle River, New Jersey
Columbus, Ohio

Library of Congress Cataloging in Publication Data

Hoffner, Helen
   The elementary teacher's digital toolbox / Helen Hoffner.
     p. cm.
   Includes index
   ISBN 0-13-170956-9
1. Elementary school teaching—Handbooks, manuals, etc. 2. Classroom management— Handbooks, manuals, etc. 3. Lesson planning—Handbooks, manuals, etc. I. Title.

LB1555.H68 2007
372.1102—dc22
                                                                                                          2006003621

Vice President and Publisher: Jeffery W. Johnston
Executive Editor: Debra A. Stollenwerk
Assistant Development Editor: Daniel J. Richcreek
Editorial Assistant: Mary Morrill
Production Editor: Alexandrina Benedicto Wolf
Production Coordination: GGS Book Services
Design Coordinator: Diane C. Lorenzo
Cover Designer: Jason Moore
Cover Image: Super Stock
Production Manager: Susan W. Hannahs
Director of Marketing: David Gesell
Senior Marketing Manager: Darcy Betts Prybella
Marketing Coordinator: Brian Mounts

This book was set in Garamond by GGS Book Services. It was printed and bound by R.R. Donnelley & Sons Company. The cover was printed by Phoenix Color.

Copyright © 2007 by Pearson Education, Inc., Upper Saddle River, New Jersey 07458. Pearson Prentice Hall. All rights reserved. Printed in the United States of America. This publication is protected by Copyright and permission should be obtained from the publisher prior to any prohibited reproduction, storage in a retrieval system, or transmission in any form or by any means, electronic, mechanical, photocopying, recording, or likewise. For information regarding permission(s), write to: Rights and Permissions Department.

Pearson Prentice Hall™ is a trademark of Pearson Education, Inc.
Pearson® is a registered trademark of Pearson plc
Prentice Hall® is a registered trademark of Pearson Education, Inc.
Merrill® is a registered trademark of Pearson Education, Inc.

Pearson Education Ltd.   Pearson Education Australia Pty. Limited
Pearson Education Singapore Pte. Ltd.   Pearson Education North Asia Ltd.
Pearson Education Canada, Ltd.   Pearson Educación de Mexico, S.A. de C.V.
Pearson Education–Japan   Pearson Education Malaysia Pte. Ltd.

10 9 8 7 6 5 4 3 2 1
ISBN: 0-13-170956-9

To my mother, Gloria, and my sisters, Gloria Ann and Nancy, who encouraged me to answer the school bell when it rang.

Teacher Preparation Classroom

MERRILL PRENTICE HALL

See a demo at
www.prenhall.com/teacherprep/demo

Your Class. Their Careers. Our Future. Will your students be prepared?

We invite you to explore our new, innovative and engaging website and all that it has to offer you, your course, and tomorrow's educators! Organized around the major courses pre-service teachers take, the Teacher Preparation site provides media, student/teacher artifacts, strategies, research articles, and other resources to equip your students with the quality tools needed to excel in their courses and prepare them for their first classroom.

This ultimate on-line education resource is available at no cost, when packaged with a Merrill text, and will provide you and your students access to:

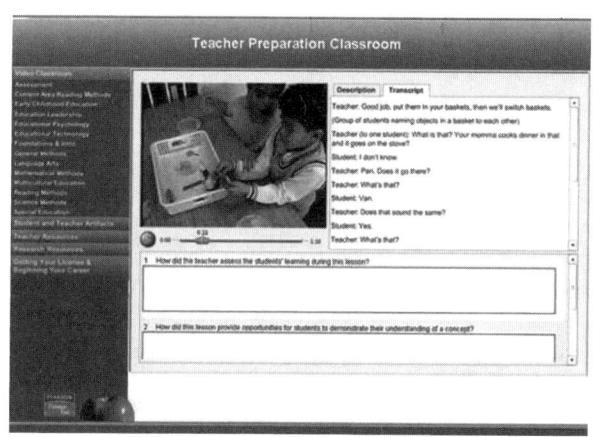

Online Video Library. More than 150 video clips—each tied to a course topic and framed by learning goals and Praxis-type questions—capture real teachers and students working in real classrooms, as well as in-depth interviews with both students and educators.

Student and Teacher Artifacts. More than 200 student and teacher classroom artifacts—each tied to a course topic and framed by learning goals and application questions—provide a wealth of materials and experiences to help make your study to become a professional teacher more concrete and hands-on.

Research Articles. Over 500 articles from ASCD's renowned journal *Educational Leadership*. The site also includes Research Navigator, a searchable database of additional educational journals.

Teaching Strategies. Over 500 strategies and lesson plans for you to use when you become a practicing professional.

Licensure and Career Tools. Resources devoted to helping you pass your licensure exam; learn standards, law, and public policies; plan a teaching portfolio; and succeed in your first year of teaching.

How to ORDER *Teacher Prep* for you and your students:

For students to receive a *Teacher Prep* Access Code with this text, instructors **must** provide a special value pack ISBN number on their textbook order form. To receive this special ISBN, please email **Merrill.marketing@pearsoned.com** and provide the following information:

- Name and Affiliation
- Author/Title/Edition of Merrill text

Upon ordering *Teacher Prep* for their students, instructors will be given a lifetime *Teacher Prep* Access Code.

PREFACE

New teachers enter their first classrooms with optimism, fear, and excitement. They wonder whether they are truly prepared and if they will be able to gain the respect and cooperation of their colleagues and students. They have been encouraged by their faculty advisors, yet they continue to search for guidance.

The Elementary Teacher's Digital Toolbox, a book and CD set, supports novice teachers with practical advice on topics such as classroom management, lesson planning, standards, assessment, diversity, inclusion, and professional development. *The Elementary Teacher's Digital Toolbox* can be used as a core text for classroom discussion, as a supplemental text for field-based courses, or as an independent study guide. It is appropriate for novice teachers, student teachers, certification candidates in induction programs, and career changers considering a move to education.

The templates on the accompanying CD enable users to customize and print materials such as reading logs, lesson plan forms, letters to parents and guardians, checklists for classroom management, review and maintenance sheets, and homework logs.

The Teachers' Resources section at the end of the book provides valuable lists of resources that teachers can use at every stage of their career. *The Elementary Teacher's Digital Toolbox* can help new teachers find success in their first classrooms.

ORGANIZATION OF THE TEXT

The Elementary Teacher's Digital Toolbox is divided into ten chapters, which move sequentially from setting goals for the first days of school to professional development and opportunities beyond the classroom. Each chapter opens with questions to ponder and ends with reflection questions.

At the conclusion of every chapter is a classroom anecdote section entitled "My Teacher Said. . . ." These are true stories that teachers have shared so that others can learn from their experiences. The stories can be discussed in student teaching seminars (or in new-teacher induction meetings) so participants can apply their knowledge and skills to actual classroom situations.

Chapters 1 through 4 help beginning teachers set goals and move into their first classrooms. These introductory chapters offer guidance on how to structure a safe and effective learning environment, initiate communication with parents, and establish professional relationships with colleagues. Chapters 5 through 7 address techniques for classroom management, explain standards, and give practical advice on lesson planning and daily activities. Chapter 8 considers the role of elementary teachers in the special education process and issues of diversity and inclusion. Chapter 9 helps teachers develop an assessment plan to monitor instruction. Chapter 10 offers thoughts on the certification process and professional development. This final chapter encourages the new teacher to participate in collegial activities within the school, such as Teachers' Book Clubs, and professional organizations, including the International Reading Association (IRA) and the National Council of Teachers of Mathematics (NCTM).

The Teachers' Resources section offers directories of standards, professional organizations, periodicals for educators, sources of free classroom materials, and websites for elementary teachers.

With a variety of topics and time-saving templates, *The Elementary Teacher's Digital Toolbox* welcomes and guides novice and student teachers as they enter the teaching profession.

USING THE CD

The book and the CD are designed to be used together. For example, Chapter 7 describes and explains the use of review and maintenance sheets to help children maintain skills throughout the school year. Teachers can then use the template on the CD to create these sheets for their own classrooms. The icon appears throughout the book to tell readers that related materials can be found on the CD.

New teachers spend hours creating homework forms, reward certificates, and letters to parents/guardians. While this work is essential, their time would often be better spent interacting directly with students and colleagues. The CD helps free teachers from routine paperwork and enables them to focus upon instruction.

The Elementary Teacher's Digital Toolbox helps student teachers and novice teachers reflect and learn from their work in the classroom. It puts the experience and advice of veteran teachers into the hands of novices and guides new teachers as they meet the challenges of their first classrooms.

ACKNOWLEDGMENTS

I have been able to write this text because many talented and generous teachers have shared their knowledge and friendship with me. My colleagues at Holy Family University have always supported my efforts. Dr. Kathleen Benson Quinn and the faculty of the Holy Family University Reading Clinic have been mentors, cheerleaders, and friends throughout the journey. Dr. June Hairston-Brown and the faculty and students of Main Line Academy have given me a venue to practice my craft and have shown me that every child can learn when he or she has a skilled and knowledgeable teacher.

When I stepped out of the classroom, many professionals at Merrill/Prentice Hall guided me in bringing this manuscript to teachers. I am grateful to Ben Stephen for his creativity in organizing this project and to Debbie Stollenwerk, Mary Morrill, Linda Bishop, and Hope Madden for providing their expertise and motivating support. Special thanks are offered to those professionals who reviewed the manuscript and offered insightful comments for revision: Linda F. Balog, SUNY, College at Brockport; Lois K. Draina, Marywood University; Joyce W. Frazier, University of North Carolina, Charlotte; Randa A. Gick, Arizona State University; Sharon L. Gilbert, Southern Illinois University, Carbondale; Dennis M. Holt, University of North Florida; Ellen Jane Irons, Texas Woman's University; Honor Keirans, Chestnut Hill College; James Kelly, University of Northern Iowa; Douglas MacIsaac, Stetson University; and Edie L. Norlin, The Ohio State University at Newark.

I owe special gratitude to my parents, George and Gloria Hoffner, who proudly told everyone that their young daughter, who played school with her dolls, was going to be a teacher. This manuscript began when they bought me my first box of chalk and persuaded my sisters, Gloria and Nancy, to enroll in my backyard school.

Helen Hoffner

ABOUT THE AUTHOR

Helen Hoffner is Associate Professor of Education at Holy Family University in Philadelphia, Pennsylvania, where she teaches graduate and undergraduate classes in reading and language arts instruction and supervises student teachers. During her career Dr. Hoffner has been an elementary teacher, a reading specialist, and the director of a school for students with learning disabilities. She has chaired school evaluation teams for the Middle States Association of Colleges and Schools and has presented workshops for parent and teacher organizations across the country. Her work as a consultant for public and private schools enables her to visit classrooms and collaborate with teachers on innovative projects.

Helen Hoffner is the author of two additional books for elementary teachers, *A Look at Realistic Fiction* and *Writing and Reading Mysteries in Grades 4 to 7*. Her articles on elementary and special education have appeared in *The Reading Teacher, Teaching PreK-8, New Teacher Advocate, Journal of Visual Literacy*, and other professional journals.

BRIEF CONTENTS

	Introduction	xxi
1	Setting Goals	1
2	Getting Ready	5
3	Structuring the Environment: Moving into Your First Classroom	19
4	The First Day of School	27
5	Classroom Management	37
6	Standards	53
7	Daily Activities and Lesson Planning	59
8	Diversity and Inclusion	79
9	Assessment and Recordkeeping	87
10	Certification and Professional Development	99
	Teachers' Resources	117
	Index	159

CONTENTS

Introduction	xxi

1 Setting Goals   1

Questions to Ponder   1
Opening Thoughts   1
Inclusion, Literacy, and Technology Goals   1
My Teacher Said . . . Anecdotes for Classroom Reflection and Discussion   3
    The First Day of School   3
Lingering Thoughts   4

2 Getting Ready   5

Questions to Ponder   5
Opening Thoughts   5
Working With the Principal   5
Working With the Faculty   6
Preparing for a Substitute Teacher   6
    The Substitute Teacher's Resource Folder   7
Greeting Your Students and Their Families   8
Knowing the Community   8
    Knowing the Community: a Study of Ridley Park, Pennsylvania   13
My Teacher Said . . . Anecdotes for Classroom Reflection and Discussion   16
    A Hairy Story   17
Lingering Thoughts   17

3 Structuring the Environment: Moving into Your First Classroom   19

Questions to Ponder   19
Opening Thoughts   19
Creating a Safe and Effective Learning Environment   19
    Questions to Address After the Students Arrive   21
Using and Storing Materials Safely   22
My Teacher Said . . . Anecdotes for Classroom Reflection and Discussion   24

Guilty or Innocent?   24
Lingering Thoughts   25
References   25

4 The First Day of School   27

Questions to Ponder   27
Opening Thoughts   27
Setting Goals   27
Getting to Know Your Students   28
    Assess Students' Strengths and Needs: Writing Samples   28
    Encourage Everyone to Participate   29
Introduce Yourself!   32
    Biography—Every Life Tells a Story   32
    The Old College Try—Activities for the Classroom   33
My Teacher Said . . . Anecdotes for Classroom Reflection and Discussion   35
    A Ringing Response   35
Lingering Thoughts   36
References   36

5 Classroom Management   37

Questions to Ponder   37
Opening Thoughts   37
Maintaining a Positive Classroom Atmosphere   37
    Speak to Every Child Every Day   37
    Watch Your Language   38
    Display Every Student's Work   38
    Maintain Order in the Classroom   38
    Give Clear Directions   39
    Be Consistent   39
    Maintain Routines   39
Establishing Routines   39
    Arrival Procedures   39
    Taking Attendance   39
    Morning Routine   40
    Collecting Homework   40
    Dismissal Procedures   40
    The Lineup   40
    Hall Passes   41

Rewards and Consequences   42
    Appropriate Rewards   42
    Inappropriate Rewards and Consequences   43

Establishing Rules   44

Why Did It Happen? Examining the Causes of Behavior   45
    Reflection/Interpretation   46

Observing Behavior   46

Share Good News With Families   48

My Teacher Said . . . Anecdotes for Classroom Reflection and Discussion   49
    Stealing Rewards   49

Lingering Thoughts   51

References   51

6 Standards   53

Questions to Ponder   53

Opening Thoughts   53

Setting the Course for Instruction: A Guide to Understanding Standards, Benchmarks, Objectives, and Curriculum   53
    The Differences Between the Curriculum and the Standards   54
    Benefits of Standards-Based Instruction   55

Implementing Standards-Based Instruction   55
    Sequence for Using Standards-Based Instruction   55
    Displaying Standards in the Classroom   56
    Explaining Standards to Parents   56
    Standards Directory   56

My Teacher Said . . . Anecdotes for Classroom Reflection and Discussion   57
    What Did They Learn?   57

Lingering Thoughts   58

7 Daily Activities and Lesson Planning   59

Questions to Ponder   59

Opening Thoughts   59

Protecting Instructional Time   59

Daily Routines   60
    Morning Messages   60
    Speaking Opportunities for Your Students   60
    Classroom Diary   60

Review and Maintenance   60

Homework 63
    Homework Folders 64
    Homework Schedule 64
    Collecting Homework 66
    Homework Reminders for the Teacher 66
Lesson Plans 66
    Writing Measurable Objectives 67
    Sample Lesson Plans 69
Thematic Units 72
    Sample Sixth Grade Thematic Unit: The Blues:
    Blending Music, Research, and Literature 72
My Teacher Said . . . Anecdotes for Classroom Reflection and Discussion 76
    Collecting Homework 77
Lingering Thoughts 78
References 78

8 Diversity and Inclusion   79

Questions to Ponder 79
Opening Thoughts 79
Students With Special Needs: Your Role in the IEP Process 79
Considerations for Diverse Classrooms 81
    Roll Call 81
    Selecting Seats 82
    Speaking Clearly 82
Media Access 82
    Captioned Programming 82
    Described Programming 83
    Audiobooks 84
My Teacher Said . . . Anecdotes for Classroom Reflection and Discussion 84
    No Hats Allowed 85
Lingering Thoughts 86
References 86

9 Assessment and Recordkeeping   87

Questions to Ponder 87
Opening Thoughts 87
Writing Samples 87
    Elementary Grades Writing Sample Collection 88

Rubrics   89
    Sample Fifth Grade Social Studies Assignment Sheet and Rubric   90
Keeping Records   91
Reading Logs   93
    Log 1   94
    Log 2   94
    Log 3   96
    Log 4   96
My Teacher Said . . . Anecdotes for Classroom Reflection and Discussion   96
    The Brightest in the Class   96
Lingering Thoughts   98

10 Certification and Professional Development   99

Questions to Ponder   99
Opening Thoughts   99
Certification   99
    The PRAXIS Series: Assessments for Certification   100
    Maintaining Certification   101
    National Board Certification   101
Substitute Teaching   102
    Pros and Cons of Substitute Teaching   102
    When the Phone Rings: Being Prepared   103
    Engaging Activities   104
    The Substitute's Summary   106
Professional Development   106
    A Word Wall for Teachers   107
Book Clubs for Teachers   108
    Organizing a Teachers' Book Club   108
    Suggested Book Club Titles   109
    Choices Booklist: Great Books to Share With Students   112
Opportunities Beyond the Classroom   113
    Tutoring   113
    Educational Publishing   114
    Field Testing Opportunities   114
My Teacher Said . . . Anecdotes for Classroom Reflection and Discussion   114
    A Favorite Book   114
Lingering Thoughts   115
References   115

Teachers' Resources   **117**

   A: Directory of Standards   **118**

   B: Directory of Professional Organizations   **124**

   C: Directory of Professional Journals and Periodicals   **131**

   D: Directory of Free Materials for Teachers   **143**

   E: Directory of Resources for Inclusive Classrooms   **149**

   F: Directory of Websites for Elementary Teachers   **153**

Index   **159**

INTRODUCTION

You have been a student most of your life. From your preschool experiences to your days at the college or university, you have sat in a student's desk and relied upon the guidance of your teachers. Now it is your turn to be the teacher. Expectant faces will turn to you to structure their day, plan assignments, and establish a comfortable classroom atmosphere. Take out this book and CD on long days when reports are due and you have little time to prepare for classes, parent-teacher conferences, and special activities. The many forms, lesson plans, and checklists will save you time and help you to meet your responsibilities in a professional manner.

As a teacher you will be making decisions that will affect the feelings and learning of children. That power comes with an obligation to build your professional knowledge and develop effective classroom management. The school principal, veteran teachers, office staff, parents, and students will provide encouragement—but they will also challenge you to climb the mountain instead of settling on the plateau. Accept the challenge, begin your climb, and rise to the peak.

Chapter 1

SETTING GOALS

Questions to Ponder

1. What are my goals for this teaching experience?
2. What talents and skills do I bring to teaching?

Opening Thoughts

You've studied, visited many classrooms, and have earned a placement as a novice or student teacher. Now it is time to focus upon your immediate goals for a specific classroom assignment and group of students.

Take time from your busy schedule of completing paperwork and gathering supplies to reflect upon your goals for the next phase of your professional life. By setting goals you gain a clear sense of your destination and the road you must take to get there. During the days before classes begin, find a quiet moment to develop priorities and complete the goal sheets found in this text. *The Teacher's Goal Sheet* (Figure 1-1) helps you reflect upon and discuss your general concerns for entering your first classroom. Figure 1-2, *Setting Inclusion, Literacy, and Technology Goals*, reminds you to focus upon these areas throughout all of your interactions with students and colleagues. By developing your goals, you chart a path for success. Review your goal sheets periodically to assess your progress and steer your work accordingly.

INCLUSION, LITERACY, AND TECHNOLOGY GOALS

Inclusion, literacy, and technology are central concerns for all educators; teachers must establish goals in these areas when they enter a new classroom.

Our students represent diverse cultures and need educators who are sensitive to unique customs and beliefs. It is also a teacher's duty to help students develop respect for cultures other than their own and to help students learn to function in a pluralistic society.

Regardless of subject area expertise, all teachers should consider the literacy needs of their students and help them to acquire necessary vocabulary and reading skills to succeed in content area instruction.

THE TEACHER'S GOAL SHEET

My new teaching assignment:

School _____ Grade Level _____
Number of Students _____

1. My central goal for this assignment is to:

   I can accomplish this goal by taking these steps:

2. My greatest challenge during this assignment will be to:

   I can meet this challenge by taking these steps:

3. When I say goodbye to my students at the end of this assignment, I hope they will say:

FIGURE 1-1
An electronic version of this material can be found in Chapter 1 of the CD.

SETTING INCLUSION, LITERACY, AND TECHNOLOGY GOALS

I will make inclusion, literacy, and technology integral parts of my instruction.

1. I will increase my students' respect for diverse needs and cultures and make my classroom an inclusive, welcoming environment by:

2. I will enhance the literacy skills of my students by:

3. Technology brings challenges as well as opportunities to the classroom. To improve my use of technology in the classroom, I will:

FIGURE 1-2
An electronic version of this material can be found in Chapter 1 of the CD.

Technology brings new opportunities to the classroom and teachers must constantly upgrade their skills to make the best use of available equipment.

By focusing upon the areas of inclusion, literacy, and technology, teachers can create an emotionally safe, welcoming environment and provide effective, positive instruction.

Use the worksheet in Figure 1-2 to reflect upon and record your goals in the areas of inclusion, literacy, and technology.

MY TEACHER SAID Anecdotes for Classroom Reflection and Discussion

Teachers need content knowledge as well as the wisdom and common sense to handle the daily crises that occur in a classroom. The following anecdote describes a surprise that greeted a new teacher on her first day of school. Read and discuss this tale with your colleagues. What advice would you give to this new teacher?

The First Day of School

On the first day of school, teacher Nicole Catania entered the classroom excitedly. She had spent the summer making learning centers, writing lesson plans, and arranging bulletin boards. She was prepared for her new role as a teacher. After reading the state's standards and benchmarks for first-grade instruction, she was confident that the lessons she had planned on phonemic awareness and basic addition facts would address the needs of her incoming first-grade students.

As the children entered the classroom and found their seats, Nicole approached a little girl named Madison who had a book in her hands. "What book do you have?" asked the new teacher. "*Junie B. Jones, First Grader at Last*," said Madison. "My dad just gave me this book. Last year I was in kindergarten and I read lots of books about Junie B. Jones and her kindergarten teacher. Now my dad says I am ready to read about the things Junie B. Jones does when she is in first grade, just like me." "That's terrific," said Nicole. "You will soon be learning how to read that book." "But I can read it now," said the child and she began reading the first page aloud.

Nicole's confidence began to fade. "I've been planning lessons on initial consonants and this child is already reading chapter books," she thought. She walked to the back of the classroom to meet more of her students. "You have lots of pencils," said a little girl as she pointed to a box on Nicole's desk. Reading the child's name tag, Nicole smiled and said, "Well, Carly, those are prizes. Students who follow the rules and work very hard can earn these special, shiny pencils." "Did you really bring sixty pencils for us?" asked Carly as she glanced at the number on the side of the box. "Yes," answered Nicole "There are twenty children in this class and I want everyone to try to earn pencils." "Then we can each get three pencils," said the little girl. Nicole was surprised that the child could divide the pencils so quickly. "If there were eighty pencils," asked Nicole, "how many could each child earn?" "Four," answered Carly. "Suppose there were ninety pencils?" asked Nicole. Carly responded quickly. "Then we could still each get four and you would have ten left over."

Nicole was bewildered. The school year had barely begun and already she had to adjust her lesson plans and her expectations. She thought she knew what to expect from first graders. She wondered whether all of the children were as advanced as the two she had just met! What could she do to determine everyone's needs?

Questions

1. How can the teacher determine the students' instructional levels?
2. What techniques can the teacher use to differentiate instruction?
3. Where could the teacher find resources to help her plan instruction?

Lingering Thoughts: A Time for Reflection

1. Have I set realistic goals for the development of diversity, literacy, and technology in my classroom?
2. At the end of this classroom experience, what techniques should I use to assess the progress I have made in meeting my goals?

Chapter 2

GETTING READY

Questions to Ponder

1. How can I make a good impression on my new principal, mentoring teachers, my students, and their families?
2. How can I learn more about my students and their families?

Opening Thoughts

You will soon enter a new school building to begin your first assignment as a student teacher or novice teacher. When you enter, you will be greeted by the school's principal, mentoring teachers, and other professionals such as the reading specialist, speech therapist, or nurse. These individuals are part of your new team. They want you to succeed because you are their partner in helping children reach their academic and social potential.

Before entering the school, take time to consider the questions you have for each of your new colleagues as well as for the parents and guardians of your students. Make appointments with members of the school community to introduce yourself and to learn their expectations for you.

WORKING WITH THE PRINCIPAL

Ideally, your principal views his or her role as a "teacher of teachers." The principal should be an experienced educator with the knowledge, skills, and determination to guide new teachers to success in their classrooms. You should welcome the principal's visits to your classroom as an opportunity to receive feedback and learn from a veteran.

Begin your school year on a positive note by meeting early and often with your school's principal. Use the questions in Figure 2-1 to help structure your meeting.

> **QUESTIONS TO ASK THE PRINCIPAL BEFORE CLASSES BEGIN**
>
> 1. Is there a faculty handbook?
> 2. How are daily updates communicated? Will I have a mailbox in the office where other faculty members, students, and parents can leave messages? Are messages posted on a school website? Does the principal send e-mail messages to the faculty?
> 3. What are my responsibilities concerning noninstructional duties such as supervising the recess yard or helping students board their buses?
> 4. Whom should I consult when a student is not making appropriate progress?
> 5. When will I receive a list of my students' names and contact information (addresses, telephone numbers, e-mail addresses)?
> 6. May I contact my students and their families with a letter, telephone call, or e-mail message to introduce myself and learn about their interests?

FIGURE 2-1
An electronic version of this material can be found in Chapter 2 of the CD.

WORKING WITH THE FACULTY

Your first year as a novice teacher or student teacher can be stressful. When meeting with mentoring teachers and colleagues in the school, remember to be flexible and listen more than you speak. Develop a good working relationship by asking questions (Figure 2-2) and learning how your skills and talents can fit with the needs and routines of the school.

Use the questions in Figure 2-2 to guide your first meetings with mentoring teachers in your new school.

PREPARING FOR A SUBSTITUTE TEACHER

There will be days when professional or family responsibilities prevent you from being in the classroom. With preparation and clear directions from you, a substitute teacher can engage your students in meaningful work to further their skills while you are away.

Your principal may require you to submit an emergency substitute teacher's plan to the school office. In addition to the lesson plan in the office, it would also be helpful to keep additional resources in a designated location

QUESTIONS TO ASK MENTORING TEACHERS BEFORE CLASSES BEGIN

1. Regularly scheduled meetings will help us remain focused on our goals. Can we establish a schedule for meetings?
2. Is there a lesson plan format you would like me to use?
3. When should I present my lesson plans to you?
4. What responsibilities will I have outside of the classroom? Will I be expected to assist with tasks such as cafeteria supervision or playground supervision?
5. What types of contact should I have with the families of my students (i.e., e-mail notices, newsletters, and phone calls)? (You and your colleagues should coordinate communication so that families do not receive conflicting information.)

FIGURE 2-2
An electronic version of this material can be found in Chapter 2 of the CD.

in your classroom to help the substitute teacher and your students enjoy a productive day.

The Substitute Teacher's Resource Folder

Prepare a resource folder for a teacher who may be substituting in your classroom. Tell your principal, a fellow teacher, and/or your students where the substitute teacher will be able to find the folder (such as in a desk drawer or file cabinet).

The Substitute Teacher's Resource Folder

- **Schedules**
  Place typical daily and weekly schedules in the folder. The schedules should contain times for activities such as the lunch period, library visits, computer lab instruction, and dismissal.

- **Student List**
  The folder should include a list of the students' names and special concerns such as students with allergies or other medical conditions.

- **Dismissal Information**
  Give the substitute teacher the information he/she will need to see that every student arrives home safely. This list might include procedures for walking students to their parents' cars or the names of students who ride the school bus.

♦ **Read-Aloud Selections**

Primary Grades
When you are absent, your students can find comfort with familiar literary figures. If your students enjoy read-aloud sessions with literary characters such as Junie B. Jones, Amelia Bedelia, Cam Jansen, or Jigsaw Jones, consider leaving another episode of their adventures for a substitute teacher to read to the class. The students will enjoy listening to the next exploit of their heroes and they will have the background knowledge to discuss the characters and settings with their substitute teacher.

Suggested Texts:
Junie B. Jones, First Grader, One-Man Band by Barbara Park
Cam Jansen and the Mystery of Flight 54 by David A. Adler
The Case of Hermie the Missing Hamster: A Jigsaw Jones Mystery by James Preller

Upper Elementary Grades
In the upper elementary grades, students may enjoy following the exploits of series characters such as Sherlock Holmes. Short mystery stories that students can solve or inspirational tales of famous Americans are also appropriate for the upper elementary grades.

Suggested Texts:
The Adventures of Sherlock Holmes by A. Conan Doyle
Five-Minute Mini-Mysteries by Stan Smith

Complete the form in Figure 2-3 and place it in a folder to guide substitute teachers.

GREETING YOUR STUDENTS AND THEIR FAMILIES

As you are preparing materials and getting ready to move into the classroom, your future students and their families are wondering about you, their new school schedule, and academic requirements. Ease the concerns of your future students and their families by sending a brief introductory letter a few weeks before the school year begins. This text contains many other letters you can customize to fit your needs. In addition to sample introductory letters, there are also interest surveys and welcoming letters you can mail to the families of incoming students. (See Figures 2-4 to 2-11.)

KNOWING THE COMMUNITY

You enter the school building each day with a great deal of content knowledge to impart to your students. How much do you know, however, about the area in which you will be teaching? Do your students have access to a

WORKING WITH SUBSTITUTE TEACHERS

A Welcome to the Substitute Teacher

Good Morning! Thank you for working with my students today.

In this packet you will find:

1. A copy of our usual daily and weekly schedule
2. A list of students with allergies and other medical concerns
3. Information on dismissal procedures
4. Selections for read-aloud sessions

If you have questions during the school day, my colleague, _____, in room _____ has agreed to help you. Feel free to turn to this colleague if you need assistance.

In addition to teaching, I have other responsibilities during the school day that you must assume during my absence. You are to take responsibility for:

(The teacher should check the appropriate category and fill in the time periods.)

_____ hall monitoring from _____ to _____

_____ bus duty from _____ to _____

_____ recess yard supervision from _____ to _____

_____ cafeteria supervision from _____ to _____

_____ other _____

I am proud of my students and hope you will enjoy your time with them. Thank you again for your help.

Best wishes,

_____

FIGURE 2-3
An electronic version of this material can be found in Chapter 2 of the CD.

public library? Are there nearby universities that can provide resources such as tutoring services or mentoring programs? Is there a YMCA that offers after-school or weekend programs? To understand the needs of your students and to assign appropriate homework and special assignments, it is

LETTER 1: LETTER TO INTRODUCE A STUDENT TEACHER TO PARENTS/GUARDIANS

Dear Parents/Guardians:

    I am proud to serve as a student teacher in your child's classroom this semester. For many years I have been attending classes, observing instruction in elementary schools, and meeting with my professors and mentor teachers to prepare for a career in education. Now I am ready to apply what I have learned to help your child meet his/her goals.

    I am completing a degree in _____ at _____ (College/University). With the supervision of your child's teacher, _____, I will be writing and implementing lesson plans, accompanying the class on assemblies and field trips, and helping to maintain an effective, positive classroom environment. I will be working in your child's classroom each day from _____ to _____ (give dates). I hope that during this time I will have an opportunity to meet you and share information about your child's progress.

    Thank you for supporting my growth as a teacher. I look forward to beginning a unique learning experience.

                                                Sincerely,

                                                _____

FIGURE 2-4
An electronic version of this material can be found in Chapter 2 of the CD.

---

helpful to understand the world in which they live. Take time to explore the community in which you teach. As you walk or drive through the area, consider the following:

- **Library Access**
  Do the students in your school have access to a public library? Does the library have computers with Internet access that are available for public use? As you tour the community, take time to enter the library to examine the resources that are available to your students.

- **Recreational Activities**
  What types of recreational activities are available in the community? Is there a YMCA or community center that offers sports or other recreational opportunities? Are there bike trails and areas to swim or fish? Learning about

LETTER 2: LETTER AND INTEREST SURVEY FOR THE STUDENTS

Dear Students,

    Wow! A new school year will be starting very soon and I just learned that I will be your teacher. This is the first year that I will be teaching in your school so I would like to introduce myself. I graduated from _____ and I now live in _____. My hobbies include _____. When I am not in school I like to _____. I love to read and I especially enjoy _____ books.

    I'd like to know more about you so that I can select books and activities that you will like. I've included a set of questions with this letter. Please answer the questions and mail them back to me at the address listed on the bottom of the sheet. I'll read your answers and plan exciting events for our year together.

    I look forward to meeting and sharing adventures with you.

                                                  Your teacher,

                                                  _____

FIGURE 2-5
An electronic version of this material can be found in Chapter 2 of the CD.

the area's recreational activities can help you understand the special interests of your students. You might also find stress-relieving activities such as yoga classes, aerobics programs, or adult sports leagues that will lead to your own enjoyment and well-being.

- **Transportation**
  Do most students walk to school or do they ride a school bus? Consider transportation needs when planning after-school or weekend events for your students and their families.

- **Corporate Benefactors**
  Have major employers such as an automobile manufacturer, large retail store, or food distributor established a presence in the community? By knowing the major employers of an area, a teacher can gain insight into the schedules and needs of the students' families as well as the resources

STUDENT INTEREST SURVEY

Student's Name _____ Age _____

Please answer the questions below so that I can learn about you and plan activities that you will enjoy.

1. How long have you been going to _____ School?
2. Do you have any brothers or sisters? What are their names and ages? _____
3. Do you have any pets? What is your pet's name? _____
4. What sports do you like? _____
5. Do you belong to any sports teams? _____
   If yes, please name the teams. _____
6. Do you belong to any other clubs or groups such as Boy Scouts or Girl Scouts? _____
7. What do you like to do when you are not in school?
8. What types of books do you like to read?
9. What is your favorite book?
10. What do you like best about school?

Please return this form to: _____
_____
_____

FIGURE 2-6
An electronic version of this material can be found in Chapter 2 of the CD.

that are available in the community. Corporations often become good neighbors by granting their employees time to volunteer in area schools or by donating cash and supplies to local classrooms.

♦ **University Resources**

Is there a university in the community? Students who are majoring in elementary education may wish to visit your school to observe in a classroom or to complete student teaching requirements. Professors who are testing innovative instructional materials or methods may wish to engage in research projects with teachers in the elementary school. Visit the education department of a local university to explore the possibilities of a partnership.

LETTER 3: LETTER AND INTEREST SURVEY FOR THE PARENTS/GUARDIANS

Dear Parents/Guardians:

Welcome to the start of an exciting school year. I look forward to getting to know you and your child and helping your child reach his/her academic goals.

I am a graduate of _____ and I hold teaching certification in the areas of _____. My special interests beyond the classroom include _____. I have included two survey forms with this letter so that I can learn more about you and your child. The student interest survey asks you to describe the hobbies, sports, and special events your child enjoys. This information will help me select books and activities that will appeal to your child. Throughout the year there will be many opportunities for your child to share his/her special talents with our class. I also hope that many of you will visit our class to discuss your career with the students, share a special hobby or talent, or serve as a guest reader. I have also included a survey sheet with this letter so that you can indicate your interest in visiting our classroom. Please return the forms to me at the address listed on the bottom of each sheet.

Frequent communication will enable us to monitor the progress of your child and ensure that he/she is receiving the most effective instruction and reinforcement. Please feel free to contact me at any time with questions or concerns. You can reach me by telephone at _____ or by e-mail at _____.

Thank you for your support of our school programs. We can work together to create a nurturing environment for the academic and social growth of your child.

Sincerely,

_____

FIGURE 2-7
An electronic version of this material can be found in Chapter 2 of the CD.

Knowing the Community: A Study of Ridley Park, Pennsylvania

Knowledge of the community can enable you to enrich the curriculum by adding local names and anecdotes when your students are studying historical events. It can help you understand the traditions and the sentiments of your students and their families. In the borough of Ridley Park, Pennsylvania, for example, many community events center around the railroad. Ridley Park was established

TELL ME ABOUT YOUR CHILD!

Child's Name _____

Parent/Guardian _____

1. What does your child like to do when he/she is not in school? List the after-school/weekend activities in which your child participates such as Boy Scouts/Girl Scouts, sports teams, or 4-H activities.
2. Does your child have additional hobbies?
3. Does your child like to read at home?
4. What types of books does your child select from the library?
5. What is your child's favorite book?
6. What is your child's favorite subject in school?
7. Is there a subject in school that your child does not like or has found to be difficult?
8. Is there anything else you would like to tell me about your child?

Please return this form to: _____
_____

FIGURE 2-8
An electronic version of this material can be found in Chapter 2 of the CD.

VISIT OUR CLASSROOM!

Everyone has a special skill or talent to share with young people. We invite parents/guardians as well as other family members and neighbors to visit our classroom to extend our learning and present new ideas to our students.

Would you like to visit our classroom to teach us a new skill, show pictures of a special trip, or discuss your hobby? If you are able to visit, we would gladly welcome you to our classroom.

Please use the form attached to indicate the special interests/talents that you would like to share with us. I will contact you to discuss a presentation for our classroom.

Thank you for your help.

FIGURE 2-9
An electronic version of this material can be found in Chapter 2 of the CD.

CLASSROOM VISITORS

Your Name: _____

Student's Name: _____

Relationship to the student: _____

Your telephone number: _____

Your e-mail address: _____

What is the special skill or talent you would like to share?

_____

_____

How would you like to present this information to the class?

(There are _____ students in our class. Would you like to work with the whole class or should the students be divided into small groups?)

List the supplies or equipment you will need.

(overhead projector, DVD player, construction paper, or other items)

Please return this form to:

_____

_____

FIGURE 2-10
An electronic version of this material can be found in Chapter 2 of the CD.

in 1887 as a summer vacation area by employees of the Pennsylvania Railroad. Trains left Philadelphia each day to bring vacationers to Ridley Park's lake and beautiful Victorian hotel and guest houses.

By the 1960s Ridley Park had become a year-round residential area and the Ridley Park station master Claude Alphin hosted special events at the train station. He often invited school and community choral groups to come to the station and sing for passengers as they boarded trains for their jobs in Philadelphia. Every December Claude put on a Santa costume, rode into Ridley Park on a train, and distributed candy canes to children waiting at the station. Claude began a tradition in which children in Ridley Park visit Santa Claus at the train station each year rather than in a shopping mall as do the children in other communities.

Since 1887, the train station has been the place where residents of Ridley Park get their news, post public announcements, and meet and greet friends. Teachers in Ridley Park understand the importance of the railroad in this community and plan interdisciplinary projects with railroad themes.

LETTER REQUESTING SUPPLIES

Dear Families and Friends,

While our school is rich with talented faculty members and volunteers, there are times when a few extra supplies would help us accomplish our goals. Many households and offices discard items such as magazines and used printer cartridges, which can help our educational program. The list below contains some items our school can trade for educational equipment as well as some items that we can use directly in our classrooms. Please examine the list and consider sending these items. Our faculty and students will appreciate your efforts.

Items Our School Can Trade for Educational Equipment:
- Labels from Campbell's products
- General Mills Box Tops for Education (found on cereal boxes as well as other items)
- Used printer cartridges

Items Our School Can Use Directly in Our Classrooms:
- Magazines (Our primary classes use magazines to cut out pictures to reinforce the new vocabulary they are learning. Intermediate and upper grade classes use magazine pictures to inspire their creative writing.)
- Cardboard rolls from wrapping paper and paper towels (Our art classes use these rolls in many projects.)

Thank you for your help.

                                                              Sincerely,

FIGURE 2-11
An electronic version of this material can be found in Chapter 2 of the CD.

MY TEACHER SAID Anecdotes for Classroom Reflection and Discussion

A teacher can influence the social as well as the academic growth of her students. The following tale shows the way in which a teacher's words influenced the actions and emotions of an entire class. Read and discuss this anecdote with your colleagues. How would you have reacted to this situation?

A Hairy Story

It was the worst haircut of his life. Nick's mom was trying to save money, so she decided to cut his hair at home. What a disaster! Short, jagged pieces of hair stuck up in the front. There was a crooked line in the back where Nick's mom had held the razor unsteadily. Nick didn't want to return to his fourth-grade classroom until his hair grew back. However when his mom insisted that he go to school, Nick put on a baseball cap and walked down the street.

As he entered the classroom, Nick's teacher reminded him that students were not allowed to wear baseball caps in the school. "I can't take it off," he whispered, "I hate my new haircut." "I'm sure you look fine," the teacher answered, "Let me see how you look." Slowly taking off his cap, Nick could hear his classmate Carlos start to snicker. "Yikes!" said Carlos, "Nick looks . . ." "Great," said the teacher, "What a cool haircut. You're starting a new style. Hey everybody, doesn't Nick look terrific?"

The teacher intercepted the laughter with compliments on Nick's new hairstyle. Soon the giggles of the fourth graders were replaced by admiring sighs. Students stood by Nick's desk and joined their teacher in complimenting him.

Carlos observed the class' reaction and then asked, "Where did you get your hair cut, Nick? Maybe my dad will let me get my hair cut like yours."

Questions

1. How did this teacher's immediate acceptance of a student influence the actions of the students in that class?
2. How did this teacher demonstrate positive leadership?
3. How did this teacher's actions affect the classroom atmosphere?

Lingering Thoughts: A Time for Reflection

1. What have I been doing to gain the support of my colleagues (mentoring teachers, administrators, university supervisors) to help me achieve my goals?
2. Am I creating a welcoming environment for parents and other members of the community?

Chapter 3
STRUCTURING THE ENVIRONMENT: MOVING INTO YOUR FIRST CLASSROOM

Questions to Ponder

1. As you have been preparing to become a teacher, you have visited many classrooms. Which classrooms have you liked the best? What special features have made those classrooms exemplary?

Opening Thoughts

You've been given the key to your first classroom and you're ready to unpack your box of bulletin board decorations, favorite books for read-aloud sessions, tissues, and markers. STOP! Decisions such as where to place the pencil sharpener or trash can may seem trivial, but these simple considerations can affect the flow of traffic and efficiency in your classroom. Before unpacking, take time to consider school policies, the needs of your students, and the factors that will help you and your students function at your best.

CREATING A SAFE AND EFFECTIVE LEARNING ENVIRONMENT

Consider the questions that follow to help you prepare a safe and effective learning environment.

- **What are the school's policies regarding classroom organization and decorations?**

    While you may have many creative ideas for your classroom, you must first consider school rules and other factors beyond your control. Before you hang posters and arrange furniture, you should read the faculty handbook, ask the principal, or consult with other teachers to learn the school's policies regarding classroom decorations. Many schools have the following regulations:
    - Evacuation/fire drill procedures must be displayed in every classroom.
    - Exits must not be obstructed by furniture or displays.

- The windows of classroom doors should not be blocked by decorations or colorful paper. Observers in school hallways should be able to look into each classroom.
- The school's philosophy, mission statement, and standards should be displayed.

◆ **What types of whole-group activities will occur in this classroom?**

After you have considered the types of activities that you would like to implement, you can then determine whether the desks should be placed in rows, pairs, or clusters of four (table arrangement). You must seat the students so they can easily see the chalkboard, whiteboard, and video screen. As you are arranging the furniture, it may be helpful to sit in a student's desk to gain a sense of a student's view and the elements that may be distracting.

◆ **Which areas of the room will require quiet?**

Areas such as a book nook or student writing center encourage quiet reflection and should not be located near noisier group activity areas.

◆ **Which areas of the room should encourage conversation?**

Learning can be a social activity and there will be times when you want your students to engage in small-group discussions. Plan conversational spaces for activities such as literature circles, buddy reading, committee meetings, or group projects.

◆ **Can students move to the chalkboards/whiteboards easily?**

Chalkboards and whiteboards enable students to come to the front of a classroom and share their work with their peers. Bookshelves and other furniture should not block a student's access to the board. When teachers hang posters, attendance charts, and other decorative items on the boards, the writing surface is reduced and students have less opportunity to present their work at the board.

◆ **Which areas may generate trash and require cleanup supplies?**

You may wish to establish a science or art center in a tiled area of the room rather than on a carpeted surface. Trash cans should be placed in areas where trash is generated so that students are not carrying messy items across the classroom.

◆ **What is the best place to store materials such as paper, pencils, and scissors for independent student access?**

Students should be able to get the materials they need without disturbing their classmates or the teacher. Paper and other potentially combustible materials must be stored away from heat sources.

◆ **Where should confidential materials be stored?**

While students should have access to most areas of the classroom, there should be some areas that are restricted. When organizing the classroom, the teacher must designate a place for confidential materials such as students' records.

Creating a Safe and Effective Learning Environment 21

- **Where do I put the teacher's desk?**
    Traditionally the teacher's desk is placed at the front of the classroom. Many teachers, however, find that they can manage their classrooms more effectively by placing their desks at the back or side of the classroom. This gives them a better view of all activities and frees space at the front of the classroom for group activities. When organizing a classroom, it is best to consider the activities of the classroom and then select the location for the teacher's desk.

- **Is the television/DVD player positioned on a secure, permanent stand?**
    Many teachers share equipment and place televisions and DVD players on carts, which can be moved from classroom to classroom. Children should not be asked to move these carts because the heavy equipment could easily fall off the cart and cause injury.

- **Are bookshelves fastened securely to a wall?**
    Extra bookshelves may seem like a good idea for teachers who want to establish a classroom library brimming with books. However, a tall bookshelf not secured to a wall could fall and injure a child.

- **Where are the electrical outlets?**
    Which equipment (such as CD or DVD players) will require the use of electrical outlets? You can't move the outlets so you will have to consider these needs when you arrange furniture and organize learning centers in your classroom.

- **Is student artwork hung safely in the classroom?**
    Often teachers encourage students to use clothes hangers to hang mobiles in the classroom. The sharp tip of a metal clothes hanger, however, can cause many classroom accidents. Plastic hangers are a safer alternative for hanging mobiles in the classroom.

- **Are cleaning products stored in a locked drawer or closet?**
    Cleaning products such as aerosol sprays can cause harm when they are used inappropriately. Keep all cleaning products as well as art and science supplies in a locked area.

After you have considered these questions and have arranged the furniture in your classroom, use the Classroom Environment Survey (Figure 3-1) to evaluate the environment you have created.

Questions to Address After the Students Arrive

- **Are the desks and chairs at a comfortable height for each student?**
    Although the students in your class may be similar in age, they may vary a great deal in height and weight. Make certain that each student has a desk and a chair that is comfortable for him or her.

CLASSROOM ENVIRONMENT SURVEY

1. Are emergency procedures clearly displayed?
2. Are the school's philosophy, mission statement, and standards displayed?
3. Where is the teacher's desk? Is it in the traditional place at the front of the classroom or is it on the side or in the back of the classroom? Why is this the best location for the teacher's desk?
4. How are the students' desks arranged? Are the desks in a traditional pattern of rows, in a horseshoe shape, or clustered in small groups? Why is this the best possible arrangement for the students' desks?
5. Are there quiet areas to confer with children individually?
6. Are there areas for small groups of children to work together on a project?
7. Are the aisles sufficiently wide to allow an easy flow of traffic?
8. Can students write on the chalkboard easily or is there furniture blocking access to it? Are decorations taking up too much space on the chalkboard?
9. Can students get supplies such as paper, pencils, scissors, and glue independently?
10. Do students have access to the classroom library?
11. Where should student portfolios and other records be stored?

FIGURE 3-1
An electronic version of this material can be found in Chapter 3 of the CD.

- **Do any of your students have special visual or hearing needs?**
   Some of your students may have visual or hearing impairments, which require special considerations for seating. A special education teacher, school nurse, or your principal can assist you in determining the best seating for these students.

- **Have you noticed any problems caused by poor placement of objects such as trashcans, bookcases, or other furniture? How could these problems be solved?**
   One way to assess the classroom environment is by focusing upon a student and examining that student's experience in the classroom. Select one student at random and use the survey sheet in Figure 3-2 to record that student's experience in the classroom.

USING AND STORING MATERIALS SAFELY

Educators often purchase innovative art supplies or materials for science classes, which can enhance instruction. If used or stored inappropriately, however, these materials can cause harm. Art supplies, science materials, and

STUDENT CLASSROOM EXPERIENCE SURVEY

Date of Observation: _____

Time of Observation: _____

(For this exercise, report only on a brief observation period of 45 to 60 minutes.)

Grade Level: _____

Subject Area: _____

Student Selected to Observe: _____

1. Can you find examples of that child's work hanging in the classroom? (List the examples such as compositions or artwork.)
2. During the period in which you observed, did the child you were watching:
   a. Read orally
   b. Go to the chalkboard/whiteboard
   c. Work with a peer
   d. Raise his/her hand to answer a question or participate in a classroom discussion
3. Did the student leave his/her seat to get supplies? If yes, were the supplies easily accessible or could they have been moved to a more convenient location?
4. At any time during your observation, was the student's seat hidden from the teacher's view?
5. Did the student leave the classroom during your observation? If the student left the classroom, how did he ask permission to leave? Did he carry a hall pass when he left?

FIGURE 3-2
An electronic version of this material can be found in Chapter 3 of the CD.

classroom cleaning products must be purchased, stored, and used responsibly. Guidelines developed by organizations such as the U.S. Food and Drug Administration (FDA) and the Art & Creative Materials Institute, Inc. (ACMI) can assist teachers as they strive to maintain a healthy classroom environment.

◆ Consider the potential and common misuses of an item.

Cleaning products in aerosol cans or those with trigger pumps are sometimes found in classrooms. Teachers sometimes encourage students to use these products independently so that they share in the responsibility for keeping the classroom neat and orderly. While this may seem like appropriate classroom management, there are potential risks. A mischievous student could pick up a trigger spray bottle and pretend or actually spray the cleaning product into the faces of her classmates. Cleaning items should be kept in locked closets or drawers. In many instances, such products should only be used by an adult after students have left the classroom.

◆ Keep cleaning products, art supplies, and science lab supplies in their original containers.

The original packaging contains the essential safety information that may be needed in the case of accidental ingestion or misuse of the materials.

◆ Make certain that work areas in art and science classes are well ventilated.

◆ When using cleaning supplies, art materials, or science materials, protect any cuts or open wounds with appropriate gloves or bandages.

◆ Use the protective equipment specified on a product label.

Gloves, safety glasses, and masks can protect users from various hazards.

MY TEACHER SAID Anecdotes for Classroom Reflection and Discussion

While most teachers strive to be fair and open-minded, negative stereotypes can sometimes cloud our judgment. The tale below describes the events that occurred when a teacher allowed her prejudices toward a child to surface. Read and discuss this anecdote with your colleagues. How would you have handled this situation?

Guilty or Innocent?

In January, the second graders returned from their winter holiday vacation with tales of family trips, snowstorms, and the exciting presents they had received. Isabelle was delighted to show her classmates a zippered pencil case her mother had given her filled with decorative pencils, gel pens, and fluorescent markers. Isabelle removed a few favorite pencils, then tucked the pouch into her desk, and went to her math class across the hall.

When Isabelle returned to the classroom, her treasured pouch was gone. Instantly she blamed George, a boy who had been sitting in her desk during the math class. Everyone knew that George was a troublemaker. He was always hitting children in the schoolyard, making nasty remarks while the teacher was talking, and writing bad words on his desk. Isabelle, her classmates, and their teacher felt sure that George had taken the pencil case and all of Isabelle's new pens and pencils.

When George denied taking the pencil case, the teacher forced him to sit alone at the back of the classroom. The teacher continued to call George a thief in front of his peers and she told him that he would be punished until he confessed and returned Isabelle's pencil case.

The teacher would use George to show the children that those who lie and steal would be punished. The pouch was not returned and for three days George stayed in the classroom when his peers went to recess.

On the morning of the fourth day, a tearful girl, Doris, approached the teacher. "I have it," she whispered. "What do you have?" asked the teacher. "I have Isabelle's pencil case. After I took it, I felt awful but I didn't know how to sneak it back into Isabelle's desk." The teacher was shocked. Doris had always been one of the best students in the class. If any student were to cause trouble, the teacher felt sure that it would be George, not Doris.

That day George went to recess with his classmates and his teacher learned a valuable lesson.

Questions

1. What lesson did the teacher learn?
2. How do you think this teacher will handle similar situations in the future?
3. How did the teacher's suspicions about George affect the classroom atmosphere?
4. Did the reputations of Doris and George influence the teacher's actions?

Lingering Thoughts: A Time for Reflection

1. What steps have I taken to make my classroom a safe environment?
2. Has the way in which I have arranged furniture and stored materials created an efficient and safe workplace? What can I change to prevent disruptions or negative behaviors?

References

The Art & Craft Materials Institute, Inc. *What you need to know about the safety of art & craft materials.* [Brochure]. Hanson, MA: Author.

Chapter 4
THE FIRST DAY OF SCHOOL

Questions to Ponder

1. What can I do to make every student in my class feel welcomed, respected, and safe?
2. What steps can I take to encourage every student to participate in class?

Opening Thoughts

Have you always wanted to be a teacher? Did you play school when you were young and dream about the day when you would hold the keys to your own classroom? That day is here and your students are waiting.

To make a positive start, three practices are essential. It is important to set goals with your students, assess their strengths and needs, and encourage them to participate in all classroom discussions and activities.

SETTING GOALS

What do your students hope to learn this year? Are they looking forward to a special event such as a field trip, championship game, or graduation? Everyone comes to the new school year with goals and dreams.

On the first day of school, read *The Places You'll Go* by Dr. Seuss to your class. This is an inspirational book that is appropriate for all ages. *The Places You'll Go* tells students that although life will bring trials and tribulations, it is possible for everyone to find the perseverance and courage necessary to triumph over adversity. *The Places You'll Go* can motivate students to set goals for the new school year.

After reading *The Places You'll Go*, open a discussion on goals for the new school year. You could begin by sharing your goals as a teacher such as improving your use of instructional technology or forming a teachers' book club to discuss professional literature. Ask your students to tell you their goals for the school year. They may have academic goals such as making the honor role or writing for the school newspaper. The students may also mention

TIME TO SET GOALS: THE STUDENT'S TIME CAPSULE

Student's Name: _____ Date: _____

This can be a year of great adventures and triumphs but you must make a plan to succeed. Start your new academic adventure by setting goals and listing the steps you will take to achieve your goals.

1. My goal for this school year is to:

2. To achieve this goal I must take the following steps:

3. The people who can help me achieve my goal are:

FIGURE 4-1
An electronic version of this material can be found in Chapter 4 of the CD.

athletic goals such as making a varsity team or competing in regional championship games.

Distribute copies of the Students' Time Capsule sheet in Figure 4-1 to help your students write their goals. Collect and store the time capsule sheets. At regular intervals such as the end of each month or the end of a marking period, return the time capsule sheets to your students so that they can evaluate the progress they are making toward attaining their goals.

GETTING TO KNOW YOUR STUDENTS

Assess Students' Strengths and Needs: Writing Samples

Diagnostic teaching requires that you assess the strengths and needs of your students and target instruction to those areas. Wise teachers gather writing samples at the beginning of the school year. An early writing sample offers a window into a child's sense of language and sentence structure as well as his knowledge of punctuation and spelling. A handwritten sample can also help teachers assess a student's fine motor ability. Early writing samples give a teacher evidence of the progress students have made during the school year. (Additional forms and information related to writing samples can be found in Chapter 9 of this text.)

The activity included in this section, *How I Spent My Summer Vacation: A Visit to Mulberry Street!*, helps you gather writing samples to assess your students' descriptive writing ability as well as spelling and punctuation skills. "How I Spent My Summer Vacation" is the classic writing prompt that teachers give on the first day of school. Invite your students to give this tired assignment a new twist by reading and responding to the Dr. Seuss classic, *And To Think That I Saw It on Mulberry Street*.

Dr. Seuss' *And To Think That I Saw It on Mulberry Street* tells the tale of Marco who has a very ordinary walk to school each day. Rather than tell his father about his dull trip, Marco decides to enhance his tale with imaginative stories of exotic animals and dignitaries that he sees on his way to school.

Read *And To Think That I Saw It on Mulberry Street* to your students on the first day of school. Tell the students that like Marco, you too have had a quiet summer and you wish that you could invent more exciting adventures to tell your family. Invite your students to discuss their activities during the summer. Some of your students may have had great adventures while others may have had a rather ordinary routine. Everyone, however, can take their experiences and enhance them in a creative writing activity in the way that Marco did.

Tell your students that they will be writing a story in the format of *And To Think That I Saw It on Mulberry Street*. Distribute the worksheet in Figure 4-2 to help your students organize their writing.

Encourage Everyone to Participate

We are creatures of habit. Some students like to sit up front, participate in discussions, and take leadership roles in the classroom. Other students are reluctant to speak in school situations and avoid the spotlight. By using friendly activities that require everyone to speak on the first day of school, you can prevent students from falling into the habit of not participating. Activities in this section such as the Get to Know You Survey and Around the Corners will help everyone become a participant from day one.

HOW I SPENT MY SUMMER VACATION: THE ENHANCED VERSION

Student: _____ Date: _____

Facts

1. Where did you spend your summer vacation?
2. What did you see there?
3. What did you do? (for example, Did you swim every day? Did you go hiking?)

Enhancement

1. If you could have gone anywhere, where would you have gone on your summer vacation?
2. Who would you have liked to meet during the vacation?
3. What would you have liked to have seen?

FIGURE 4-2
An electronic version of this material can be found in Chapter 4 of the CD.

Get to Know You Survey

It's the first day of school and there are twenty-five to thirty new faces sitting in front of you. You know you can quickly learn their names but how will you ever get to know which students have large families, which students have traveled about the country, or which students speak more than one language? How will you ever get to know their hopes and dreams, their favorite books, or their after-school activities? Your students have many exciting adventures and special characteristics to share. Help everyone in the class learn more about each other with the Get to Know You Survey.

Copy and distribute the Get to Know You Survey in Figure 4-3. Tell the students that they will have 5 to 10 minutes to find at least one student in the class who fits the requirement for each category. Then set a timer for 5 to

GET TO KNOW YOU SURVEY

Find a student in the class who...	
	Student's Name
1. has a dog	
2. has a cat	
3. has a bird, fish, or hamster	
4. plays on a sports team	
5. has a brother	
6. has a sister	
7. rides a bus to school	
8. walks to school	
9. rides a bike to school	
10. comes to school by car	
11. is a musician	
12. likes to draw	
13. has lived in more than one state	
14. has had his/her name or picture in the newspaper	
15. has been on television	
16. has ridden a horse	

17. has traveled to another country	
18. likes math better than any other subject	
19. likes reading better than any other subject	
20. likes to cook	
21. likes to go camping	
22. has traveled on an airplane	
23. likes to play chess	
24. likes to play board games such as Monopoly or Sorry	
25. likes to sew or do crafts	
26. likes to send e-mail	
27. likes to play video games	
28. likes to surf the Internet	
29. likes to swim	
30. likes to read the newspaper	

FIGURE 4-3
An electronic version of this material can be found in Chapter 4 of the CD.

10 minutes. Allow the students to walk about the classroom to talk to their classmates and complete the survey. The students should return to their seats when the timer rings.

Some classes may have students who are unable to read the survey independently. In these situations teachers may wish to read the entire survey aloud with the class before asking the students to work independently. Struggling readers could also be paired with a stronger reader to complete the activity.

Ask the students to share their results with the entire class.

Around the Corners

Get everyone out of their seats on the first day of school by asking them to take a stand on an issue that affects the entire class.

1. Select an issue the class has the power to decide such as determining the destination or date for a field trip or choosing due dates for book reports. Present four options to your students. (Example: The class could take a field trip to a museum, factory, newspaper office, or another school.) Then ask each student to select one option.

2. Designate one corner of the classroom for each option and ask the students to stand in the corner that represents their choice. (Example: Students choosing to go to the museum would stand in the right front corner of the classroom. Those who wish to go to the factory would stand in the left front corner. The students who have selected the newspaper office would go to the right back corner and the students who wanted to visit another school could stand in the right back corner.)

3. Tell the students that the class must reach consensus. Each group must use their powers of persuasion to convince their classmates to leave their respective corners and join them.

4. This activity forces every student to take a stand and participate. No one can remain in his seat to watch the action.

INTRODUCE YOURSELF!

Biography—Every Life Tells a Story

Share your life with your students and help them understand the literary genre of biography/autobiography.

1. Bring pictures, yearbooks, and additional mementos of your elementary and secondary school experiences to share with your students. Describe the schools you attended and explain the reasons why you decided to become a teacher.

2. Tell the class that you would like to put your story in writing. Define the terms *biography* and *autobiography* and ask the class if they have read any biographies or autobiographies. Encourage the students to discuss their favorite biographies.

3. Use a chalkboard, dry erase board, or large chart paper to show the children how to begin writing an autobiography. Use a type of "think-aloud" process as you begin to jot ideas to include in your autobiography. Encourage the children to help you add descriptive words and phrases.

4. When you have a brief rough draft of an autobiography, invite the children to think about their own life stories. Tell the class that they will also have an opportunity to write their autobiographies.

5. Tell the children that you will schedule several additional class sessions in which they can develop their autobiographies. Encourage the children to discuss this project with their families. Family members may be able to contribute photographs and give the children ideas to include in their autobiographies.

The Old College Try—Activities for the Classroom

You are a new face in the classroom and the students sitting before you wonder about your background and your interests. The students may have been told that you are a student teacher or that you recently graduated from a local college or university but they probably know very little about the school you attended. Share facts about your college or university to help your new students learn more about you and to motivate them to prepare for their own college days.

College 101: Introduction to College

1. Begin the lesson by entering the classroom wearing a sweatshirt or tee shirt representing your college or university. You may also wish to bring a college pennant to hang in the classroom.
2. Use a KWL (What I Know, What I Want to Know, What I Have Learned) chart to guide a discussion on college life. To make a KWL chart, make three columns on the chalkboard or on large chart paper.

K	W	L
What I Know	What I Want to Know	What I Have Learned

Ogle, D.M., 1986

3. Ask the students for their impressions about college. How long does it take the average student to earn a bachelor's degree? How many classes does a full-time student take each semester? What type of homework does a college student have? As the students answer questions and share their thoughts, write their contributions in the K, What I Know, column of the chart.
4. Ask the students if they have questions about college. What would they like to know about college life? Write their questions in the W, What I Want to Know, column.
5. Use a college course catalog, website, and other publications to answer your students' questions. Help your students write the facts they have learned in the L, What I Have Learned, column of the chart.

Sports Scene

Build your students' reading skills by encouraging them to follow the progress of your college's or university's sports teams in the newspaper. Bring a newspaper to class and explain the parts of the newspaper as you turn to the sports section. Show a headline and read an article about one of your school's sports teams. Tell the students that you will continue to bring the newspaper to school on a regular basis so that the students can read about each game that team plays. The students could also develop their skills in technology by following the progress of the team on the Internet. Invite athletes from your college or university to visit your classroom to give the students an extra treat.

Grade Point Average (GPA)

Children wonder whether college students take tests and get report cards like they do. Discuss the grading system at your college with your students. Develop a sample student roster and show the students how your college determines a grade point average (GPA). Depending upon the age of your students, you may be able to create math problems asking them to determine a grade point average.

Sample: College Student: Joe Freshman Fall Classes/Grades			
Course Title	Credits	Grade	Points
History of Education	3	A	4.0
World Literature	3	B	3.0
Mathematics	3	A	4.0
Geography	3	B	3.0
American History from 1776 to 1860	3	A	4.0
Credits attempted: 15	Credits earned: 15		GPA: 3.6

More College Math

Use a college course catalog to create additional mathematics problems for your students.

College Math Problem Examples:

1. Full-time students at most colleges and universities take 12 to 18 credits each semester. Ask your students to use a course catalog to select a history course, a mathematics course, and electives that will result in 12 to 18 credits. Your students can use the worksheet given on the next page to list the courses they have selected.

STUDENT WORKSHEET EXAMPLE:

Course	Credits
	Total Credits =

2. Attending college costs money. Help your students gain an understanding of college costs by calculating the cost of tuition, room, and board for one semester. Your students can research these costs and compare rates at various colleges and universities by using course catalogs and the Internet.

MY TEACHER SAID Anecdotes for Classroom Reflection and Discussion

Often teachers don't realize the impact that their quick remarks can have on impressionable students. The following tale shows the way in which a teacher's passing remark affected one little boy. Read and discuss this anecdote with your colleagues. What would you have done in this situation?

A Ringing Response

From the moment he entered kindergarten, Brian was fascinated by the school's Bell Choir. He watched them perform at school events and looked forward to the day when he would be old enough to join. Finally on a September Tuesday afternoon when Brian was in fifth grade, the school's music teacher, Miss Leedy, stepped into Brian's classroom and invited students to join the Bell Choir. "Ask your parents to sign the permission form," said Miss Leedy, "and return the form to me by Thursday." Brian took the form home and smiled as his father signed it.

That evening Brian returned to the school to attend a Boy Scout meeting. On his way to the meeting, he stopped at the music room and slid the signed permission form under the door. He knew that Miss Leedy was very strict about deadlines and he wanted to be sure that she received his form by Thursday.

When classes were over on Wednesday, Brian sat on the school steps and waited for his mother's car. He hoped that Bell Choir practices would start soon. He looked forward to wearing a red robe and performing for his parents and younger sister, Hannah. Brian's mother soon pulled into the schoolyard. She parked the car and stepped out to open the trunk.

As Brian was walking to the car, Miss Leedy came outside. "Miss Leedy," called Brian, "I left my Bell Choir permission form under your classroom door last night. Did you get it? Do you have it?" Miss Leedy turned and said, "Brian, you have to grow up and be responsible for your own things. I can't keep track of papers from every student. I don't remember whether I got your form and frankly this is not the time to be asking me about it." Miss Leedy walked to her car, put her tote bag in the back seat, and drove away. She never greeted or made eye contact with Brian's mother who had overheard the conversation.

Brian got into his car and slunk into the backseat beside his sister. "I'll come to school and talk to Miss Leedy tomorrow," said his mother. "It's just a misunderstanding. I'll ask her if she received your form." "Don't bother," said Brian, "Just forget it. I don't want to be in the Bell Choir."

Questions

1. How did this teacher's response affect the student's interest in participating in an activity?
2. Did the student approach the teacher appropriately?
3. Did the teacher address the student appropriately?

Lingering Thoughts: A Time for Reflection

1. Did every student feel comfortable participating in our initial activities together? What can I do to encourage more participation?
2. What have the initial activities helped me to learn about my students?

References

Ogle, D. M. (1986). K-W-L: A teaching model that develops active reading of expository text. *The Reading Teacher, 39,* 564–570.

Chapter 5
CLASSROOM MANAGEMENT

Questions to Ponder

1. What steps can I take to create an effective learning environment?
2. How can I make my classroom an emotionally safe environment for everyone?

Opening Thoughts

A wise parent once said, "I like to visit schools at the end of the day and watch the expressions on the faces of the teachers. Do they look tired and frazzled? Have they been worn down by the stress of their responsibilities? I want my child to have a teacher who leaves school each day in a positive frame of mind—tired perhaps, but feeling satisfied that they have spent the day with my child productively."

MAINTAINING A POSITIVE CLASSROOM ATMOSPHERE

Everyone wants to wake up each morning and go to a place where they will feel welcome, respected, and confident. The classroom should be a safe haven. It should be a place in which students feel comfortable reading orally, completing math problems at the chalkboard, participating in discussions, and raising their hands to ask questions. Students cannot learn when they feel anxious and worry that they will be embarrassed in front of their peers. Effective classroom management reduces stress and enables teachers and students to focus upon the curriculum.

The reminders that follow will help you maintain a positive classroom atmosphere.

Speak to Every Child Every Day

Sadly some students have very few supportive adults in their lives. There may be no one in their homes to engage them in conversations about their school work or to watch them play on a team. Teachers should make an effort to speak to every student every day.

Stand at the classroom door during the morning arrival, afternoon dismissal, and during the change of an instructional period. Speak to every child every day even if it is only with a comment such as, "Your hair looks great today, Maya," or "Good luck on your math test, Josh."

Plan daily activities that require students to speak to their classmates. Group projects and morning meetings can force all students to speak to their classmates.

Watch Your Language

Teachers sometimes unintentionally upset a child with seemingly innocent comments such as "This is easy" or "Anyone can do it." A task may seem easy to an adult who has mastered the necessary skills. When a child is struggling, however, telling him the task is easy and that everyone else can do it causes him greater anxiety.

Display Every Student's Work

Teachers should display at least one work sample from every child. Primary teachers should also make certain that each child's name is displayed in the classroom.

Maintain Order in the Classroom

An effective, positive classroom should hum. While most students need a quiet atmosphere to learn, absolute silence at all times is usually not recommended. A classroom visitor should hear the low murmur of students working in groups, the shuffling of papers, and the reassuring calm voice of the teacher. Teachers should be able to maintain order and a purposeful hum with the techniques that follow.

Proximity

Proximity is a key factor in maintaining order in the classroom. Teachers can lessen a student's disruptive behavior by standing next to that student's desk, thereby letting the student know that the teacher is aware of her actions.

Circulation

A teacher usually cannot maintain classroom order by sitting behind a desk. Effective teachers constantly move about the classroom to monitor their students' work.

Whisper Rather Than Shout

Many teachers raise their voices when their students talk inappropriately. Whispering, however, is often more effective than shouting. When the teacher responds to noise by speaking in a soft voice, the students will usually stop their talking to hear what the teacher is saying.

Give Clear Directions

Students can be more productive when they know the amount of time they will have to complete assignments and when they know the teacher's expectations. Whenever students are given an assignment, they should also be given the rubric by which they will be evaluated.

Be Consistent

Effective teachers establish rules with their students and enforce those rules consistently.

Maintain Routines

Unexpected changes can cause stress, which leads to inappropriate behavior. Whenever possible, teachers should develop a consistent schedule of classroom routines and deviate from that schedule as little as possible.

ESTABLISHING ROUTINES

Arrival Procedures

Each school has procedures for assuring that students arrive safely and are supervised at all times. Consult your faculty handbook or your principal to learn:

- The time that teachers are expected to be in the school building

- The time that teachers assume responsibility for their students
    In some schools, students who arrive early are supervised by paraprofessionals. New teachers need to know the time when student supervision becomes their responsibility.

- The place where students report when they arrive at school
    In some schools students remain outside in the school yard until their teacher greets them. Other schools direct students to an inside waiting area such as a cafeteria or gymnasium.

Taking Attendance

When students leave their homes, parents assume that they will walk to school or ride the school bus and arrive at school on time. Many schools ask parents to call each morning if their children will be late or absent. Teachers must take attendance each morning and notify administrators immediately when students are absent.

Morning Routine

A positive, productive morning routine sets the tone for the entire school day. Students should have a routine task to complete as they enter the classroom and await the morning instructional period. Making entries in a daily journal, recreational reading, or copying homework would be appropriate independent activities to start the day.

Collecting Homework

Teachers should establish a system for collecting homework. Nothing is more frustrating for parents than to watch a child complete his homework at night but forget to give it to the teacher the next day. Uncollected homework assignments can quickly accumulate in the bottom of a child's backpack or at the back of his desk. Collect homework each day and keep a record of all completed assignments. Notify parents promptly when students become delinquent in their assignments.

Dismissal Procedures

Students in the primary grades need reminders to pack the books and materials they will need to complete their homework. List the necessary materials on the chalkboard or call out each item as the children pack their bags.

New teachers should ask the principal and fellow teachers the following questions concerning dismissal procedures:

- What time should students pack their schoolbags and prepare for dismissal?
- Where do children assemble to ride the school bus?
- Where do car riders assemble?
- Are dismissal procedures announced each day on the school's public address system?
- Where should a child wait when his parents are late in picking him up?

Use the transportation form in Figure 5-1 to compile a list showing the names of children who walk home from school, those who will ride home in a car, and those who will ride each school bus. Keep this list in a desk drawer, taped inside a closet, and/or in a folder with information for substitute teachers. **This list should not be posted in an area where the general public can see it and learn which children will be walking home, riding school buses, etc.**

The Lineup

TV shows and movies often show a teacher standing at the front of a line leading her students down the hall to an assembly, the cafeteria, or recess. While this image seems appropriate on film, experienced teachers know that they cannot

TRANSPORTATION CHART

Enter each student's name in the appropriate column. This list should be kept in a teacher's drawer or emergency folder. *It should not be displayed in an area with public access.*

Bus 1	Bus 2	Bus 3	Bus 4	Students who will be picked up by car.	Students who will walk home from school.

FIGURE 5-1
An electronic version of this material can be found in Chapter 5 of the CD.

manage a line by standing at the front with their backs to the students. When escorting a class down the hall, teachers should walk near the middle of the line or at the back of the line. Those viewpoints enable a teacher to monitor behavior and to make certain that all students reach the destination safely and orderly.

Hall Passes

Occasionally students will request permission to leave the classroom individually. Consult your faculty handbook or ask the principal to explain the procedures in your school. Some schools insist that students always travel in pairs. Many schools require students to carry a hall pass (Figure 5-2) when they are in the halls during instructional periods.

HALL PASS

Hall Pass	Hall Pass
This student, _____, has permission to travel to _____	This student, _____, has permission to travel to _____
Teacher	Teacher
Date	Date

FIGURE 5-2
An electronic version of this material can be found in Chapter 5 of the CD.

REWARDS AND CONSEQUENCES

To maintain a positive atmosphere in the classroom, teachers should focus upon rewarding desired behavior rather than punishing inappropriate behavior.

Reward or penalize students for actions that are within their control. A kindergarten student usually has no control over what time he arrives at school and should not be punished for lateness. An eighth grade student who lives within walking distance to the school, however, can usually be held responsible for arriving at school on time.

Appropriate Rewards

- **Extra Time With the Teacher**
  Spending lunchtime with the teacher can be a special reward rather than a consequence for inappropriate behavior. Students can earn lunch with the teacher by completing assignments well, showing special consideration for classmates, or by volunteering for service projects in the school or community.

- **Extra Computer Time**
  Students who complete their work efficiently can earn extra time on the computer to play educational games or to use graphics programs to make cards, posters, and personalized items.

- **Reward Bookmarks**
  Attractive bookmarks can be given to students as a reward for a job well done. (See Figure 5-3.)

Inappropriate Rewards and Consequences

- **Snacks**
  Avoid using snacks such as candy or cookies as rewards. Teachers should promote healthy lifestyles and should not use food as a reward for good behavior.

BOOKMARK REWARDS

Copy this bookmark template onto heavy colorful paper and distribute bookmarks to your students as a reward for work well done.

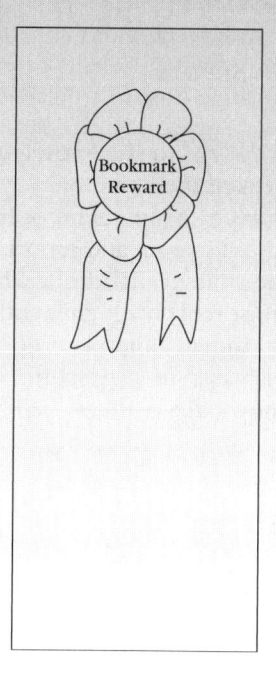

Bookmark Reward

FIGURE 5-3
An electronic version of this material can be found in Chapter 5 of the CD.

- **Written Assignments**
  If teachers want their students to enjoy writing, written assignments cannot be used as punishments. The student who misbehaves should not be asked to write a 500-word essay on the inappropriateness of her behavior. Such an assignment causes a student to see writing as a disagreeable chore rather than an exciting form of communication.

- **Corporal Punishment**
  Corporal punishment such as striking a child with a paddle is illegal in most areas of the United States. While most teachers would never hit a child, many teachers do not realize that other seemingly more benign acts can also be classified as corporal punishment. Demanding that a student stand for a prolonged period of time or requiring a student to write an excessively long assignment can be considered corporal punishment. Not only are such punishments ineffective, but in many cases they are illegal and a teacher giving these punishments could face dismissal, loss of certification, and criminal charges.

- **Depriving a Student of a Class in a Specialty Area such as Art, Music, or Physical Education**
  Art, music, and physical education are instructional areas of the curriculum rather than special privileges. There are skills to be learned and teachers in those areas must meet with their students on a regular basis. We wouldn't deprive a misbehaving student of math class so why should we take away a physical education class or art class?

- **Sending a Student to the Principal's Office**
  Teachers weaken their credibility when they send defiant students to the principal's office. In a moment of frustration, a teacher might say, "That's it! Leave this classroom and report to the principal's office!" Such an action tells the student that the teacher cannot handle classroom management and must rely on a higher authority. It also presents the danger that the defiant student might not go to the principal's office but instead roam other parts of the school or leave the building without the teacher's knowledge.

ESTABLISHING RULES

Effective teachers establish rules with their students and enforce those rules consistently. You will enter your first classroom with a general idea of the rules you believe are necessary to maintain an effective, positive classroom environment. These rules will have been shaped by your own school experiences, observation of your mentoring teachers, and discussions and readings that took place in your college coursework.

CLASSROOM CONTRACT

As a student in room _____ of _____ School, I will follow the rules of my classroom. These rules have been explained, discussed, and agreed upon by my teacher(s) and classmates. If I do not follow the rules, I will accept the consequences that have been explained to me.

_____   _____
Student Signature   Date

_____   _____
Teacher Signature   Date

_____   _____
Teacher Signature   Date

_____   _____
Witness   Date

FIGURE 5-4
An electronic version of this material can be found in Chapter 5 of the CD.

While you may have an outline of the classroom rule system you would like to use, you should develop the final set of classroom rules and consequences collaboratively with your students.

A sample classroom contract you can adapt with your student is given in Figure 5-4.

WHY DID IT HAPPEN? EXAMINING THE CAUSES OF BEHAVIOR

When a disruption or inappropriate behavior occurs in the classroom, wise teachers investigate the causes and use their findings to prevent more problems. An ABC approach (Antecedents-Behavior-Consequences) helps teachers evaluate the cause of a student's disruptive behavior and find effective responses (Kazdin, 2005; Mueller, Jenson, Reavis, & Andrews, 2002).

Factors such as the time of day, an uncomfortable seating arrangement, or instructions that are too advanced or too simplistic can influence behavior. For example, inappropriate behavior often occurs immediately before the lunch break because the students are tired, hungry, and in need of a change of pace. Negative behavior can be the result of seating arrangements that put too many students in a small area. Many students misbehave when they are placed in

WHY DID IT HAPPEN?
EXAMINING THE CAUSES OF BEHAVIOR

1. Describe the student's inappropriate behavior in the second column, the Behavior column.
2. In the first column, the Preceding Events column, list the events that immediately preceded the student's inappropriate behavior (i.e., Was the student challenged by a peer? Did the student receive a low grade on an assignment?).
3. In the third column, the Consequences column, list the consequences the student faced for the inappropriate behavior (i.e., Did the student lose a privilege such as recess or extra time on the computer?).

Preceding Events	Behavior	Consequences	Teacher's Comments

FIGURE 5-5
An electronic version of this material can be found in Chapter 5 of the CD.

classes that are too difficult. Other students become inattentive and cause disruptions when the instructional material presented is beneath their capabilities.

Figure 5-5 contains a chart teachers can use to record and examine inappropriate behavior.

Reflection/Interpretation

1. Study the data recorded on the table to find trends that led to the inappropriate behavior (i.e., Did the student misbehave every time he was asked to read orally? Did the disruptions occur when there was an abrupt change in the schedule?).
2. How did the student react to the consequences? Were the consequences effective? The consequences must be changed if the inappropriate behavior continued.

OBSERVING BEHAVIOR

"Marie is constantly out of her seat, always talking, and never listening to directions. She gets into more trouble than any other child in my classroom!"

Teachers strive to have positive relationships with all of their students. Occasionally, however, a teacher may become frustrated when she feels that one student seems especially disruptive or disrespectful. At these times it is helpful to step back and assess inappropriate behavior objectively. The observation sheet that follows can be used to help teachers understand and reflect upon the causes for unacceptable behavior in their classrooms.

Begin by selecting two children in your class, one who seems disruptive and one who appears to be following the classroom rules. In the Behavior column, list appropriate behaviors for students in your class and list the inappropriate behaviors you attribute to the disruptive child. Observe the two children during a class period and make a tally mark each time you notice one of the targeted behaviors.

You may wish to observe the two children during a period in which another teacher is instructing the class (such as an art or music period) or when you have the assistance of a classroom aide. The additional adult in the classroom would free you of your normal responsibilities and enable you to concentrate on the behavior of these two children. Examine the sample chart and then use the blank chart found in Figure 5-6 to record the behavior of students in your classroom.

OBSERVING BEHAVIOR

	Student's Name	Student's Name
Appropriate Behavior		
Inappropriate Behavior		

FIGURE 5-6
An electronic version of this material can be found in Chapter 5 of the CD.

OBSERVING BEHAVIOR SAMPLE CHART

	Student's Name Marie Nercoff	Student's Name Gloria James
Appropriate Behavior		
Raising her hand to answer a question or participate in a discussion	X X	X X X
Assisting another student appropriately	X	X X
Inappropriate Behavior		
Talking when the teacher is giving directions	X X X	X X X
Leaving her seat without permission	X X	X X X X

In the sample above, the teacher felt that Marie Nercoff's classroom behavior was disruptive. By objectively comparing Marie Nercoff's behavior to that of another student, however, the teacher came to realize that Marie Nercoff's behavior was actually similar to that of a student whom the teacher felt was following classroom rules.

SHARE GOOD NEWS WITH FAMILIES

Many parents dread phone calls and notes from their child's teachers. For them, a message from the teacher means that their child has broken a school rule or is not making satisfactory academic progress. Effective teachers establish positive communication by catching a child being good and reporting that good behavior to parents and guardians (Figure 5-7). When appropriate actions are noticed and rewarded, children are encouraged to continue to act in the desired manner.

GOOD NEWS NOTICE!

Good News to Announce to the Family of

_____

The above named student has excelled today and has made me proud to be a teacher. Here's what this student has done:

_____

_____

_____

_____

_____

FIGURE 5-7
An electronic version of this material can be found in Chapter 5 of the CD.

MY TEACHER SAID Anecdotes for Classroom Reflection and Discussion

Through their daily interactions with classmates and teachers, children learn that their actions have consequences. The following tale shows that while rules and discipline are important, forgiveness is also essential for growth. Read and discuss this tale with your colleagues. How would you have handled this situation?

Stealing Rewards

Kate's second grade teacher, Mr. Davis, had a great reward system. The students could earn Davis Dollars by completing their homework, performing special acts of kindness, or showing extra good behavior. Every Friday the students traded their Davis Dollars for stickers, pencils, and small toys in the classroom store.

One Friday Kate brought 18 Davis Dollars to the classroom store to purchase a stuffed animal. This puzzled Mr. Davis. Most of the students had earned approximately 10 Davis Dollars during the week and Kate should have had less than the average amount because she had not completed all of her homework. Suddenly Mr. Davis remembered that a few children had complained that Davis Dollars had been disappearing from their desks. Mr. Davis hadn't worried about the missing Davis Dollars. He thought those students had simply miscounted or lost the certificates in their desks. Now he wondered if their Davis Dollars had actually been stolen. "How did you get so many certificates, Kate?" asked Mr. Davis. "Don't you remember?" replied Kate, "You gave me extra dollars because my homework was very neat." Mr. Davis knew that wasn't true but he hesitated before accusing this student. "We'll talk about this later," he said, "Come and see me after lunch."

That afternoon Kate approached her teacher. "How did you get so many Davis Dollars?" asked Mr. Davis. "I earned extra dollars during math class and during recess," answered Kate. "Many children have told me that their Davis Dollars are missing," said the teacher. "Do you know what happened to them?" "No," answered Kate. "How did you get so many Davis Dollars?" the teacher asked again. Finally Kate began to cry. "I took some," she whispered. "I saw lots of them sticking out of Samantha's desk so I took two and I thought she wouldn't notice. Then I took more from Wally's desk on Tuesday when he was absent."

"You weren't being fair to your friends, Kate," said the teacher. "Your friends worked hard to earn their Davis Dollars and you stole them. Give me the Davis Dollars. You won't get a prize today."

Mr. Davis told the class that he was closing the school store for the day because he needed to add more prizes. He would open the store again on Monday.

On Monday Mr. Davis paid special attention to Samantha and Wally as they completed math problems at the chalkboard. "You've done terrific work," he said and he gave them extra Davis Dollars. During recess the teacher spoke privately with Kate. "I won't tell your classmates what happened," he said, "You and your parents can meet with me after school tomorrow and we'll find a solution."

Kate did not have an opportunity to earn Davis Dollars during the next two weeks. As the school year progressed, however, she earned rewards with her classmates. No more Davis Dollars were reported stolen.

Questions

1. This teacher decided not to publicly embarrass or accuse his student. Do you agree with his decision?
2. How would you have resolved this problem?
3. How did this teacher's actions affect the classroom atmosphere?

Lingering Thoughts: A Time for Reflection

1. Which techniques have helped me to encourage positive behavior and maintain a comfortable learning environment for all of the students?
2. Have I consistently used positive language in my conversations with students?

References

Kazdin, A. (2005, August 22). Family therapy effective for youths, study says. *The Philadelphia Inquirer*, pp. B1, B4.

Mueller, F., Jenson, W. R., Reavis, K., & Andrews, D. (2002). Functional assessment of behavior can be as easy as A-B-C. *Beyond Behavior*, 11(3), 23-27.

Chapter 6

STANDARDS

Questions to Ponder

1. What impact do standards have in my classroom?
2. How do I find the standards that I should address?

Opening Thoughts

The No Child Left Behind Act of 2001 has brought standards and Standards-Based Instruction to the forefront of educational discussions. Teachers at every grade level are being held accountable to local and state standards as well as standards set by subject area organizations such as the National Council of Teachers of Mathematics (NCTM) and the International Reading Association (IRA). Teachers must have a thorough understanding of terms such as standards, benchmarks, objectives, and curriculum in order to join the conversation and plan instruction.

SETTING THE COURSE FOR INSTRUCTION: A GUIDE TO UNDERSTANDING STANDARDS, BENCHMARKS, OBJECTIVES, AND CURRICULUM

Standards are expectations that describe what students should know and be able to do when they have completed a program of instruction.

Benchmarks are student behaviors that demonstrate progress toward meeting a standard.

Objectives state the desired outcome for a lesson.

Curriculum is the plan of instruction offered by an individual school or school district.

Education is a journey and the **standards** are our destination. When an individual embarks on a journey, he thinks about his final goal as he wanders down the path. As a traveler, he wants to be certain that the directions he has been given are correct and that each step will take him closer to his goal. **Benchmarks** are the encouraging mileposts and landmarks that reassure the traveler that he has not veered from his course. These marks along the trail offer motivation to keep going. **Objectives** explain why the destination was selected and why it is important to go there.

Standards explain what students should know and be able to do when they complete a program of instruction (i.e., the end of a school year or high school graduation). Benchmarks are the behaviors students show to demonstrate their progress toward meeting a standard.

Objectives state a purpose for a lesson and explain why it is important for the teacher and students to spend their time in a particular activity. Objectives should be highly specific and should be written in measurable terms. For example, an objective such as "The students will learn to read" would be inappropriate for a lesson plan. Students do not "learn to read" in one lesson nor in one calendar year. Learning to read is a process in which we continually expand our vocabulary and build comprehension throughout a lifetime. An appropriate objective would be, "After reading a paragraph, the students will state the main idea of the paragraph." That is an objective that could be accomplished in one class period and could be measured (evaluated).

The Differences Between the Curriculum and the Standards

A school district or an individual school has a curriculum. The curriculum lists topics to be addressed in each subject area and grade level. For example, a school district's curriculum might indicate that fifth grade students should read a variety of literary genres. The curriculum would also give lists of approved textbooks and trade books, the amount of time that should be devoted to language arts instruction, and the assessment tools used to measure mastery of the curriculum.

Standards are not as specific as curriculum. A standard is a more general guide telling teachers what students are expected to know and do at a particular grade level. A standard might state that students should read for understanding and enjoyment. The accompanying benchmark would indicate that students should read and discuss literature. These statements do not indicate specific books or instructional techniques such as guided reading, shared reading, or buddy reading. They do not specify an assessment tool such as the Motivation to Read Profile (MRP) or the Critical Reading Inventory (CRI) for measuring the attainment of this standard. Lists of approved trade books and textbooks as well as assessment tools would be included in a school or school district curriculum guide rather than in the standards. The curriculum is a more inclusive document reflecting the philosophy and the preferred instructional techniques and materials of the school or school district.

Benefits of Standards-Based Instruction

A teacher using Standards-Based Instruction has her goals in sight. She knows why she is using specific instructional methods and materials and she can articulate her reasons to students, parents, and administrators. Standards are beneficial to the educational community because they specify the following:

- Specify exactly what students should know and be able to do as a result of instruction.
- Specify the competencies expected of teachers and students.
- Specify expectations before instruction begins and before students start their assignments. This preparation makes it reasonable and fair to assess the performance of teachers and students based on the criteria (standards) that they have been given.

IMPLEMENTING STANDARDS-BASED INSTRUCTION

Example: Reading/Language Arts Standard for Fifth Grade Instruction

Standard: Reads for understanding and enjoyment

Benchmark: Reads and discusses literature with classmates

Objective: The students will participate in a literature circle discussion of the novel, *Maniac Magee*.

Sequence for Using Standards-Based Instruction

1. Identify a standard.
2. Plan instruction to meet the standard.
3. Assess the effectiveness of your instruction.
4. Reflect upon the instruction. What worked? What didn't work? What would you do differently next time?

A new teacher is often overwhelmed when she enters her first classroom. She often has questions such as "How do I know what I should be teaching? What can I expect students to know at the beginning of fifth grade? What should they be able to do when they leave fifth grade? How will I know if they have made progress?"

In the past, teachers often based their lesson plans upon the topics and sequence prescribed by a textbook or workbook. When using Standards-Based Instruction, however, teachers begin with standards rather than topics. The standards become the guide rather than the textbook.

A fifth grade reading teacher, for example, may be given a list of 12 standards to address during the academic year. After reading the list, she may decide to focus upon three standards during each grading quarter. She would then refer to her school's curriculum to find lists of trade books she could use to address those standards.

Teachers can use a variety of tools to assess the effectiveness of their instruction. The fifth grade teacher who is asking students to read a novel might take anecdotal records when the students are engaged in literature circles. She could evaluate the effectiveness of using literature circles by recording the comments the students make in their literature circles, observing their eagerness to participate, and evaluating final projects such as a Reading Log or Reader Response Journal.

Time is a precious commodity and teachers must use the hours they spend with their students wisely. After conducting a lesson, it is vital for teachers to reflect upon the experience. Teachers should ask themselves questions such as:

- Was this lesson a success?
- If the lesson was a success, what could I do differently next time to make it even better?
- If the lesson did not succeed, why didn't it? What could I do differently next time to reach my students?

Displaying Standards in the Classroom

Many teachers are required to display local, state, or national standards in their classrooms. Writing the standards for every lesson on the chalkboard or whiteboard, however, can be time-consuming and can force a teacher to turn her back on a classroom full of active young children. To alleviate these problems, veteran teachers make posters or charts to display the standards. Some teachers write each standard on a sentence strip and then display only the sentence strip that applies to the lesson being taught. Other teachers hang a poster in their classroom listing all of the standards and benchmarks for their particular grade level.

Explaining Standards to Parents

It is also important to share these standards with your students' parents. Use Figure 6-1 to explain the standards to parents.

Standards Directory

A Standards Directory can be found in the Teacher's Resources section of this text and on the accompanying CD. This directory can help teachers locate appropriate standards for lesson planning, monitoring student progress, and professional development.

LETTER TO EXPLAIN THE STANDARDS TO PARENTS

Dear Parents,

Perhaps as you have been reading newspapers and watching news broadcasts you have encountered the term Standards-Based Instruction. Standards are expectations that describe what students should know and be able to do when they have completed a program of instruction (such as graduation or the end of a school year). In an effort to provide the most effective instruction for your children, our school has been implementing a plan of Standards-Based Instruction. When planning lessons and selecting instructional materials, I refer to the standards set by _____ (*Give the name of the state, school district, or educational organization—such as McREL—that supplies the standards you follow.*) You can find these standards online at _____ or you may examine a copy in _____ (*Give a location such as the school office or your classroom.*)

By becoming familiar with the standards, you will be able to monitor your child's progress and understand our goals. Please feel free to contact me if you would like to discuss the standards and their implications for your child's education.

Sincerely,

_____

FIGURE 6-1
An electronic version of this material can be found in Chapter 6 of the CD.

MY TEACHER SAID Anecdotes for Classroom Reflection and Discussion

Creative lesson plans motivate students and energize a classroom. While it is often exciting to close the textbook and explore hands-on activities, teachers must remember to focus upon standards and objectives. Read and discuss the following tale with your colleagues. What changes could you suggest for the teacher portrayed in this anecdote?

What Did They Learn?

Madeline Church thought that planning and implementing thematic units was one of the most interesting aspects of teaching. The textbooks she read in college suggested that the first step in planning a thematic unit was to examine the standards so that a teacher could base all instruction and assessment on those standards. Madeline, however, thought that was a very dry approach. She preferred to focus upon memorable, hands-on activities that would motivate her students.

In February Madeline planned an interdisciplinary unit to help her fourth grade students learn more about George Washington. During their reading period, the students read historical fiction selections set in colonial America. The art teacher helped the students make portraits of Washington. On February 22, Washington's birthday, Madeline read aloud the story of Washington cutting down the cherry tree. She then used her math period to guide the students as they followed a recipe and baked a cherry pie in the oven in the faculty kitchen.

At the end of the month, Madeline assessed the success of the unit by asking her students to write compositions stating what they had learned. "The cherry pie was delicious," wrote Leslie, "I learned how to make a pie crust and add filling." "It's important to tell the truth," wrote Nevin. Bernard's paper said, "I learned that when creating a portrait, it's best to begin by drawing an outline in pencil." "But what did they learn about George Washington?" wondered Madeline.

Questions

1. What were the teacher's objectives for the unit?
2. Was this a successful unit?
3. Could the teacher have based her instruction on standards and still used hands-on activities?

Lingering Thoughts: A Time for Reflection

1. What role do standards play in my classroom?
2. Have my students been able to meet the standards?

Chapter 7

DAILY ACTIVITIES AND LESSON PLANNING

Questions to Ponder

1. What types of daily routines will build community spirit in my classroom?
2. What are the elements of a successful lesson plan?

Opening Thoughts

Consistency in the classroom relieves stress, helps teachers stay on course to meet their goals, and gives students security. While an occasional surprise brightens the school day, most students find comfort in a predictable schedule and the consistent enforcement of classroom rules.

PROTECTING INSTRUCTIONAL TIME

Instructional time each day is limited and teachers must take appropriate precautions to protect the hours that they have with their students. Interruptions for schoolwide announcements and assemblies can intrude upon instructional time. When establishing a classroom schedule, consider meeting with your colleagues to establish safe or protected instructional time periods for each grade level in your school. Safe periods are instructional periods during which there are no interruptions such as schoolwide announcements or snack sales (Allington & Cunningham, 2002). During a safe period no student should leave the classroom for special services such as speech therapy or an instrumental music lesson. Scheduling safe blocks requires cooperation among all teachers and administrators in a school. The resulting increase in instructional time, however, is worth the effort and diplomacy required to establish these periods.

DAILY ROUTINES

Morning Messages

Every student deserves to begin his day in a positive, efficient atmosphere devoted to learning. Teachers can set the tone for the day with a 5- to 10-minute period to give morning messages and hold meetings with students.

Try to give all announcements at the start of the day or class period. This would be a time to greet students and invite them to share their news. A 5- to 10-minute summary of upcoming events will set a positive tone and help students plan their day. This routine will also minimize the risk of announcements disrupting valuable instructional time.

Speaking Opportunities for Your Students

Are you the sage on the stage or the guide on the side? Students need positive opportunities to speak before their classmates. Your daily routine should include at least one guaranteed opportunity for students to speak before their classmates. Suggested speaking opportunities include:

- Reading the morning announcements
- Time for students to read aloud brief excerpts from their favorite books
- Time for students to share their completed writing
- Time for students to tell a joke or share their news with classmates

Classroom Diary

Throughout the year there will be special joys, frustrations, and memorable guests in your classroom. Invite your students to help you create a classroom diary to record those events.

Place a three-ring binder with several sheets of loose-leaf paper in a corner of the classroom. Tell the class that one student each day will have an opportunity to write a diary entry. Move through the class list alphabetically giving each child an opportunity to record the day's events.

REVIEW AND MAINTENANCE

As a high school student you probably studied a second language, learned algebraic equations, and memorized formulas in chemistry. Unless you have been using this information on a regular basis, however, you may have forgotten a great deal.

Review and Maintenance

REVIEW AND MAINTENANCE SHEET

Student: _____

Subject: _____

Week of: _____

Monday	Tuesday	Wednesday	Thursday	Friday

FIGURE 7-1
An electronic version of this material can be found in Chapter 7 of the CD.

After skills are introduced, your students need regularly scheduled practice to maintain their progress. Periodic Review and Maintenance sheets[*] can help your students remember what they have learned throughout the school year.

To use Review and Maintenance sheets in your classroom:

- Examine the sample Review and Maintenance sheets in language arts and mathematics, which are provided in this text.
- Use the blank grid found in Figure 7-1 and Chapter 7 of the CD to create weekly Review and Maintenance sheets.
- Give the students review questions each day. For example, if you teach sixth grade students to find square roots in September, you should occasionally put square root problems on Review and Maintenance sheets for the remainder of the school year so that the students don't forget what they learned.

[*]The ones in this text are based on work by the Sister Servants of the Immaculate Heart of Mary.

SAMPLE REVIEW AND MAINTENANCE SHEET FOR A FIFTH GRADE LANGUAGE ARTS CLASS

Student: Eileen Baker
Subject: *Language Arts*
Week of: *October 17*

Monday	Tuesday	Wednesday	Thursday	Friday
Use this sentence to answer Monday's questions: *Juan rides the bus to school.*	Use this sentence to answer Tuesday's questions: *Every day I carry pens, pencils, and books in my schoolbag.*	Use this sentence to answer Wednesday's questions: *Across the river, I saw a beautiful castle.*	Use this sentence to answer Thursday's questions: *We went to see him win the tennis match.*	Use this sentence to answer Friday's questions: *Ryan, Nicole, and I cheerfully watched a terrific movie at the mall.*
What is the proper noun in that sentence?	Identify every common noun in that sentence.	Identify a preposition in that sentence.	Identify the pronouns in that sentence.	Identify a pronoun in that sentence.
What is the verb in that sentence?	Identify the verb in that sentence.	Identify an adjective in that sentence.	Identify the subjective pronoun in that sentence.	Identify an adverb in the sentence.
Identify a preposition in that sentence.	Rewrite the sentence by adding one proper noun.	What is the subject of that sentence?	Rewrite the sentence and replace the subjective pronoun with a proper noun.	Identify an adjective in the sentence.
What type of sentence is this? (i.e., declarative, interrogative, imperative, exclamatory)	Write one declarative sentence.	Identify a verb in that sentence.	Write an imperative sentence.	Identify the object of the sentence.
What is the subject of that sentence?	Write an imperative sentence.	Identify an adjective in that sentence.	Write a sentence with at least one adjective and one adverb.	Write one interrogative sentence.
Write a sentence containing a prepositional phrase.	Write a sentence containing at least one adverb.	Write a sentence containing a possessive pronoun.	Write a declarative sentence.	Write a sentence containing a subjective pronoun.

SAMPLE REVIEW AND MAINTENANCE SHEET FOR A FOURTH GRADE MATHEMATICS CLASS

Student: Ryan Catania
Subject: *Mathematics*
Week of: *April 9*

Monday	Tuesday	Wednesday	Thursday	Friday
2 + 28 =	32 − 4 =	>,<, or = 45 + 1 ___ 48	>,<, or = 101 ___ 110	>,<, or = 96 ___ 24 + 37
56 × 34 =	49 − 34 =	72 + 3 + 3 =	94 × 2 =	Nicole had 3 dozen apples. If there were 23 children in her class, would she have enough apples for everyone?
There are ___ items in one dozen.	There are ___ feet in one yard.	There are ___ inches in one foot.	There are ___ ounces in one pound.	There are ___ quarts in one gallon.
984 − 279 =	36 × 4 =	73 − 48 =	687 + 345 =	765 × 4 =
Nancy studied for 4 hours. How many minutes did she study?	Which is greater, 4/10 or 2/3?	39 × 45 =	967 − 288 =	Which is greater, 7/8 or 4/5?
>,<, or = 5 cups or 2 quarts	1 gallon equals ___ quarts	Which is greater, 2 hours or 135 minutes?	___ centimeters equal one meter.	2/3 + 3/8 =

HOMEWORK

No student (or his parents) welcomes an unexpected, lengthy homework assignment. Consistency and predictability is as important in homework assignments as it is in classroom instruction. Consider developing weekly homework folders so that students and their families will know your expectations and will be able to complete assignments comfortably on their own family schedule.

Homework Folders

Ask each student to bring a two-pocket folder to use as his/her weekly homework folder. Designate one day each week as the day on which you will place new assignments in the weekly homework folder. (Thursday often works well. It is near the end of the week so you can base assignments on the progress your students have made and if students or parents have questions, they can speak to you on Friday before classes are dismissed for the weekend.)

Homework Schedule

When homework is given on a consistent basis, families know what to expect and plan their schedules accordingly. At the start of the school year, make a list of the standard homework assignments you will give each week. Traditional assignments such as the study of new spelling words and math problems may be given every night. Additional assignments including book reports and social studies presentations may be given on a less frequent schedule. When you have completed a list of the assignments you will give on a regular basis, plan a schedule to include in the homework folder each week. An example is given in this text. A template you can use to create your own weekly homework schedule can be found in Figure 7-2 and in Chapter 7 of the CD.

HOMEWORK SCHEDULE
WEEK OF OCTOBER 25–29

Subject Area	Monday	Tuesday	Wednesday	Thursday	Friday
Reading	Read one chapter of the novel you selected in class and discuss that chapter with someone at home.	Read one chapter of the novel you selected in class and discuss that chapter with someone at home.	Read one chapter of the novel you selected in class and discuss that chapter with someone at home.	Write a summary of the chapters you have read. Be prepared to share your summary with your classmates on Friday.	Read one chapter of the novel you selected in class and discuss that chapter with someone at home.
Spelling	Write new words 3 × each	Use each new word in a sentence.	Use each new word in a sentence.	Study for a spelling test	
Math	Complete Worksheet 1 included in this homework packet.	Complete page 46 in the math textbook.	Complete Worksheet 2 included in this packet.	Complete Worksheet 3 included in this packet.	Complete Worksheet 4 included in this packet.

Homework **65**

Social Studies	Read pages 46-58 in the textbook.	Write a 2 to 4 paragraph summary of Chapter 3.			
Science	Remember—The Science Fair will be held on November 13. All projects must be brought to school by November 12!				

HOMEWORK SCHEDULE WEEK OF _____					
Subject Area	Monday	Tuesday	Wednesday	Thursday	Friday

FIGURE 7-2
An electronic version of this material can be found in Chapter 7 of the CD.

Collecting Homework

Have you ever peeked inside a third grader's backpack? At the bottom of the backpack there are often crumpled homework assignments, notes from teachers to parents, and field trip permission slips that were never delivered. Parents become frustrated when they watch their children complete homework each night yet fail to give it to the teacher the following day. Develop a routine for collecting homework to help students take responsibility.

Homework Reminders for the Teacher

A teacher should always consider the purpose and benefits of an assignment before giving it as homework. What will the student gain by completing the assignment? If a teacher cannot satisfactorily answer that question, then the assignment should not be given.

Never give assignments you will not check or discuss in class. Homework should give students an opportunity to try a new skill and to receive feedback on their efforts. If a student does not receive feedback on his assignment, he will never know the improvements he must make to progress to the next level nor will he have the satisfaction of knowing that he has completed a job well.

Homework should be used as a review, not as an introduction to a concept. Homework assignments should give a student an opportunity to practice a skill that has already been introduced in class. A parent may monitor homework but a family member should not be expected to directly teach new concepts.

LESSON PLANS

Planning and implementing effective lessons can be satisfying and exciting for teachers. The planning process enables teachers to use their knowledge, interests, and creativity to help students acquire new skills. Lesson planning provides opportunities to collaborate with colleagues, consult professional literature, and explore new materials. Every lesson plan is a statement of a teacher's professionalism.

Each school or district has its own lesson plan requirements. Some schools ask teachers to write weekly lesson plans, which are submitted to the principal on Monday mornings. Others require teachers to make copies of their lesson plans available to parents. While the format for each school or district varies, all lesson plans share common elements. The minimum requirements for every lesson plan are an objective, a procedure, and an evaluation. Additional information such as the time needed to complete the lesson, the materials required, and the standards to be addressed should also be included. At the end of each lesson, teachers should make reflective comments to improve their instruction.

Writing Measurable Objectives

Objectives define the lesson. They state the purpose for bringing students together and asking them to spend time with a teacher. In many ways, objectives are the most important element of the lesson plan. Without an objective the lesson has no purpose and is not worth the students' time.

Objectives should be written in terms describing the students' behavior rather than the actions of the teacher. For example, a statement such as "To distribute and introduce new trade books for the literature circles" describes the teacher's role and is not an objective for the students. A more appropriate, student-centered objective would be, "To select a trade book to read and discuss in a literature circle."

Objectives must be measurable. Measurable means that a teacher can prove to students, administrators, and parents that the students can now accomplish new tasks because of the instruction they have received. Consider the objective, "Given fractions with like denominators, the students will add the fractions." That is an appropriate objective because it is measurable and defines the expectations. To measure or prove that the students have accomplished that objective, a teacher could simply ask the students to go to the chalkboard and add fractions with like denominators. By contrast, an objective such as "The students will understand fractions" is inappropriate. It is too broad. Are the students being asked to demonstrate the basic understanding of fractions that an elementary student would have or the understanding of a mathematics professor? How can the teacher know whether the students understand fractions? Abstract terms such as understand, learn, appreciate, or know should not be used in an objective.

The Word Wall for Writing Objectives gives suggestions for appropriate verbs to use in lesson plan objectives.

A WORD WALL FOR WRITING OBJECTIVES
Appropriate Verbs to Use When Writing Lesson Plan Objectives

A	B	C	D
Acquire	Bake	Categorize	Dance
Add	Build	Check	Debate
Analyze	Buy	Classify	Defend
Apply		Combine	Define
		Compare	Demonstrate
		Compose	Design
		Compute	Detect
		Connect	Dissect
		Contrast	Distinguish
		Convert	Divide
		Cook	Draw
		Criticize	

E Equate Employ Estimate Evaluate Explain	**F** Find Fix Formulate	**G** Give Graph	**H** Hide Hypothesize
I Identify Illustrate Implement Indicate Integrate Interpret Isolate	**J** Jog Join Jump	**K** Keep Keystroke Knit	**L** Label List Locate
M Make Match Measure Mix Monitor Multiply	**N** Name Notify	**O** Observe Operate Order Organize	**P** Paint Participate Perform Plan Play Predict Prepare Program
Q Query Question Quiz	**R** Rank Read Recall Recite Recognize Repair Represent Reproduce Restate Retell Review	**S** Say Select Sequence Sing Solve State Subtract Summarize	**T** Tell Transform Translate
U Use Utilize Underline	**V** Verify View	**W** Watch Weigh Write	**X** X-ray
Y Yard Yield	**Z** Zip		

Sample Lesson Plans

Teachers can use the samples in this section to develop lesson plans that meet the needs of their students. (See Figure 7-3.)

Use the weekly planner in Figure 7-4 to help you focus upon your instructional objectives and your responsibilities within your school.

Annotated Lesson Plan Format

Lesson Plan Format

Subject Area:

Grade/Age Level: _____   **Number of Students:** _____

Lesson Title: _____

Give a title that enables your colleagues and students to know the topic and purpose of the lesson.

Time needed to complete this lesson: _____

Objective: The objective states the purpose for the lesson. It is the reason why the students are spending their time with you. Objectives should be brief, one to three sentences, and should be written in measurable terms.

Standards: To comply with the United States' No Child Left Behind Act of 2001 as well as other federal and state legislation, many teachers are now required to identify the standards they have addressed in their lesson plans. Upon accepting a new position, teachers should consult their faculty handbooks or meet with their principal to learn the standards they are expected to address and document in their lesson plans. (A directory to help teachers find state, federal, and subject area standards can be found in the Resources section of this text and on the accompanying CD.)

Materials: List all materials that will be needed to complete this lesson. Teachers who change classrooms throughout the day should list basic requirements such as pencils and paper so that they have what they need in unfamiliar environments.

Procedure: Describe exactly what the teacher and students will do to accomplish the objective.

Evaluation: Describe a method for determining whether the students have met the objective.

Reflection: Which factors made this lesson successful? Which factors impeded the success of this lesson? If you were to teach this lesson again, what would you change?

LESSON PLAN FORMAT

Subject Area:

Grade/Age Level: Number of Students:

Lesson Title:

Time needed to complete this lesson:

Objective:

Standards:

Materials:

Procedure:

Evaluation:

Reflection:

FIGURE 7-3
An electronic version of this material can be found in Chapter 7 of the CD.

WEEKLY PLANNER

Week of _____

Special assignments this week: _____ (i.e., playground duty, bus duty, lunchroom duty)

Special events this week: _____

Time/Subject	Monday	Tuesday	Wednesday	Thursday	Friday

FIGURE 7-4
An electronic version of this material can be found in Chapter 7 of the CD.

Sample Lesson Plan

Subject Area: Literacy

Grade/Age Level: Grade 3   **Number of Students:** 25

Lesson Title: A Comic Sequence

Time needed to complete this lesson: 45 minutes

Objective: Given individual frames of a comic strip, the students will put the frames in a logical sequence to tell a story.

Standards: Students place events in sequence to retell a story.

Materials

Newspaper Comic Strips (Colorful Sunday comics work best.)

Envelopes

Overhead Projector

Transparencies of Several Comic Strips

Procedure

1. Begin the lesson by asking the students to name their favorite stories. After the children have named a few stories, tell the class that stories are told in sequence or a logical order. When we retell a favorite story, it is important to retell the events in the original sequence.
2. Show the children a comic strip such as *Peanuts*. (You may wish to make a transparency of the comic strip and show it to the class on an overhead projector.) Tell the class that each frame in the comic strip tells part of the story.
3. Show the class several additional comic strips. As you discuss the comics, note the ways in which each frame of the comic strip advances the story.
4. Ask the students to work with a partner. Give each pair of students an envelope containing pieces of a comic strip, which has been cut apart. Challenge each set of students to reassemble the pieces to put their comic strip in the correct sequence.
5. After each pair has successfully assembled one comic strip, provide time for the teams of students to trade envelopes so that they can practice putting additional comics in sequence.
6. Provide time for each pair to share an assembled comic strip with the class.

Evaluation: Ask the students to place the frames of a comic strip in a logical sequence. The students should use the comic strip's frames to tell a story.

Reflection: When I introduced the lesson, I learned that many of the students do not receive newspapers in their homes and they were not familiar with comic strips. Although the children were able to put the comic frames in sequence, it would be beneficial to give them more practice with this technique. I will put complete, uncut comic strips in a classroom literacy center for the students to read independently. I will also cut some comic strips apart and put them in envelopes in the literacy center so that the students can repeat this activity independently and gain more practice in sequencing.

THEMATIC UNITS

In addition to planning daily lessons, teachers often plan thematic units that may range from one week to one month. Thematic units enable teachers to link several subject areas to provide instruction focusing upon a single topic. An example of a standards-based, thematic unit that links instruction in literacy, social studies, and music is given in this section.

Sample Sixth Grade Thematic Unit: The Blues: Blending Music, Research, and Literature

Ask your students to name rock musicians and they will eagerly raise their hands and shout out the names of their favorites. If you ask them to name classical musicians, you will probably hear the names of Beethoven and Mozart. Many students enjoy country music and can list the top country performers. How many of your students, however, are familiar with Blues music? The Blues represents a significant expression of American culture and history yet many students have only limited knowledge of Blues musicians and the development of this American art form.

Invite your students to listen to Blues selections and to reflect upon the themes presented. After listening to songs and learning the historical development of the Blues, your students can create timelines, write their own Blues lyrics, and link themes presented in songs to various works of literature.

McREL Standards addressed in this unit:

Writing

Level III

Standard 4

- Gathers and uses information for research purposes
- Organizes information and ideas from multiple sources in systematic ways (e.g., timelines, outlines, graphic representations)

Standard 2

- Uses the stylistic and rhetorical aspects of writing
- Uses descriptive language that clarifies and enhances ideas

Reading

Standard 5

- Uses the general skills and strategies of the reading process

♦ Reflects on what has been learned after reading and formulates ideas, opinions, and personal responses

Student Objectives

The students will:

1. Create timelines to show the historical development of the Blues
2. Write lyrics for an original Blues song
3. Compare themes presented in Blues songs to the themes presented in various short stories and poems

Resources/Materials Suggested

1. **Text**

    From Sea to Shining Sea: A Treasury of American Folklore and Folk Songs
    Compiled by Amy L. Cohn
    Published by Scholastic, 1993

    This is a wonderful collection of American folklore, folk songs, and poetry. The book contains literature to fit popular themes such as pioneer travel, the Revolutionary period, baseball legends, jobs in America, and modern-day Americans. The glossary of terms at the back of the book can be especially helpful to teachers preparing lessons.

2. **Websites**

    1. Blues Road Trip website

        http://www.pbs.org/theblues/roadtrip.html

        This website shows how the Blues developed in various parts of the United States. Students can visit this website to hear selections and find significant names and dates.

    2. CDB Lyrics Website (Charlie Daniels Band)

        http://www.charliedaniels.com

        Students will find the lyrics for many Blues selections at this website.

    3. Read-Write-Think Website

        http://www.readwritethink.org

        This website, sponsored by the International Reading Association, the National Council of Teachers of English, and the MarcoPolo Education Foundation, has free interactive tools for student use. Students can use the Time Line Student Interactive to complete activities in the Blues unit. The Time Line Student Interactive can be found at http://www.readwritethink.org/student_mat/index.asp

3. **Software**

    TimeLiner 5.0 published by Tom Snyder Productions
    > This program enables students to easily create timelines with graphics and captions.

4. **Music**

    Fiddle Fire: 25 Years of the Charlie Daniels Band
    > Blue Hat Records, 1998
    >
    > This collection contains songs teachers can play to introduce students to Blues music.

Introduction

In addition to developing literacy skills, this unit introduces a form of music, the Blues, which may be unfamiliar to many students. You may wish to set the mood by playing Blues selections as the students enter the classroom.

Begin the unit with a brainstorming session. Ask the class to name classical musicians, country musicians, and rock-and-roll musicians. Then ask the students to name Blues musicians. If the class is unable to name any Blues artists, tell them that the activities in this unit will introduce them to the Blues and perhaps inspire them to begin listening to this form of music. You may have students who are able to name several Blues artists and give some facts about those artists. In that situation, tell the class that these activities will help them learn more about the origins of the Blues and its popularity.

Developmental Activities

1. **History of the Blues**

    Invite the students to visit the Blues Road Trip website with you (http://www.pbs.org/theblues/roadtrip.html) to explore the history of the Blues. At this site you will find a map of the United States with points indicating four locations of significance in the development of the Blues. Use the website to play Blues selections for the class and to show pictures of Blues artists.

    1. After demonstrating the website for the class, divide the students into four groups. Assign each group one point on the Blues Road Trip map. Ask the groups to visit their assigned point on the map and to read the information contained under the history and highlights section.
    2. Ask each group to select four to eight significant dates from the historical section they read. The groups should then make a timeline showing these events. The students could make a timeline with pencil and paper or they could use a program such as Tom Snyder's TimeLiner 5.0. A free timeline maker is available at the Read-Write-Think website http://www.readwritethink.org/student_mat/ index.asp

3. Provide time for each group to share their timeline with the entire class. You might wish to help each group make a transparency of their timeline so that everyone can see and discuss each timeline.

2. **Linking Lyrics and Literature**

    Songs often remind us of favorite stories and poems. Ask each group to select one of the Blues selections they have heard and to then find a short story, novel, or poem with a similar theme. Examples:

Blues Song	Related Literature
Sweet Betsy from Pike	The Ballad of Lucy Whipple
Devil Went Down to Georgia	The Devil and Daniel Webster

3. **Writing the Blues**

    1. Give the students copies of lyrics to Blues songs such as Boogie Woogie Fiddle Country Blues, Talk to Me Fiddle, or High Lonesome. Teachers can find and print these lyrics by visiting the CDB Lyrics website:
        http://www.charliedaniels.com
    2. Play Blues songs and ask the students to follow the lyrics as they listen. Discuss the lyrics with the students. What themes can be found in these songs? Many people assume that Blues is the music of the downtrodden and depressed. Actually, Blues music takes a realistic view of human relationships and offers a sense of relief from life's daily struggles. The Blues lifts the listener from sadness and offers hope and strength.

        After hearing several songs, brainstorm possible lyric topics that might appeal to your students (examples: Lost My Homework Blues, Didn't Make the Team Blues, School on Saturday Blues).
    3. The students have learned a great deal about the Blues and now it is time for them to make a contribution. Ask the students to work in groups to write their own lyrics for a Blues song. Their lyrics should reflect their knowledge of common Blues themes and forms. The students may wish to revisit the Blues Road Trip website for inspiration and reminders of Blues themes and forms.
    4. Provide time for each group to share their song lyrics with the entire class. When each group shares their lyrics, you can also ask them to state what they have learned about the Blues during these lessons.

Student Assessment/Reflections

Throughout this unit, the students have worked in groups to build a timeline, write lyrics for Blues songs, and compare works of literature. Distribute this rubric and provide time for the students to evaluate their work.

THE BLUES: BLENDING MUSIC, RESEARCH, AND LITERATURE

	Yes/No	Comment
History of the Blues		
Did our timeline contain at least four significant dates listed in sequence?		
Did all members of our group contribute to the timeline?		
Writing the Blues		
Did our group write and share lyrics with the class?		
Did every member of our group help to write the lyrics?		
Linking Lyrics and Literature		
Did our group find stories and poems that reminded us of Blues songs?		
Did everyone participate in a discussion about the Blues songs, stories, and poems?		

Source: Kendall, J. S. & Marzano, R. J. (2004). *Content knowledge: A compendium of standards and benchmarks for K–12 education.* Aurora, CO: Mid-continent Research for Education and Learning. http://www.mcrel.org/standards-benchmarks/. Reprinted by permission of McREL.

MY TEACHER SAID Anecdotes For Classroom Reflection and Discussion

Treating students fairly includes giving clear directions and understanding their personal schedules. Read and discuss the following tale with your colleagues. Did the teacher in this situation treat his students fairly?

Collecting Homework

On Friday afternoon sixth grade student Jim McCall sat in his social studies class and watched the clock. The Memorial Day weekend would begin in a few hours and Jim and his family were going camping in the Pocono Mountains. Jim's fishing gear and sleeping bag were already packed in the family car. He had worked hard during the week to finish his assigned reading and several projects so that he could go on this trip without worrying about homework. As the social studies class was ending, however, the teacher, Mr. Herbert, wrote an assignment on the chalkboard.

"Here's your next assignment," said Mr. Herbert, "I'd like you to write a report on Pennsylvania history. Select any related topic that interests you and prepare a written report and a 5-minute oral presentation. We will not meet on Monday because the school is closed for the Memorial Day holiday, so this assignment is due on Tuesday." The bell rang and the class was over before anyone could protest or ask questions about the assignment.

Jim raced home and went straight to his computer to find information on the Internet. He printed several articles and packed them with his camping gear. Later as the family drove to the campground, Jim sat in the back seat and began his homework. Throughout the weekend Jim scribbled notes, outlined the articles, and prepared his presentation. He cut short his fishing time and hikes in the woods so that he could finish his homework by the deadline. While his brothers and sisters were swimming, Jim sat at the edge of the lake to work. During the Monday night drive home, Jim finished the rough draft of his written report. Arriving home at 8:00 p.m., he unpacked the car and typed the final copy.

On Tuesday afternoon Jim felt tired but proud that he had completed his assignment. He placed the report on his desk and waited for the teacher to collect it. "Good afternoon," said the teacher. "Today we will review chapter 8 so that you are ready for a test next week." A girl in the third row raised her hand and asked, "Aren't we going to give our oral reports? Are you going to collect the written reports that are due today?" "No," said Mr. Herbert, "I'm not going to collect anything today. I didn't explain the assignment well on Friday so I've decided to give you more time and specific guidelines. Keep the papers you wrote and revise them according to the guidelines I will give you today. The revised assignment is not due until Thursday."

Questions

1. Do you think the teacher treated his students fairly?
2. What steps could the teacher take to avoid conflicts with future assignments?
3. What policies should teachers develop for collecting homework assignments?

Lingering Thoughts: A Time for Reflection

1. If someone asked my students to describe a typical school day, what would they say?
2. Have I been using my lesson plans as helpful guides or have they become restrictive?

References

Allington, R., & Cunningham, P. (2002). *Schools that work: Where all children read and write.* Boston: Allyn and Bacon.

Kendall, J. S., & Marzano, R. J. (2004). *Content knowledge: A compendium of standards and benchmarks for K-12 education.* Aurora, CO: Mid-continent Research for Education and Learning. http://www.mcrel.org/standards-benchmarks/. Reprinted by permission of McREL.

Chapter 8

DIVERSITY AND INCLUSION

A class or grade is an abstraction; it exists in the teacher's mind or nervous system. Actually, a class is comprised of Bobby, Johnny, Mary, Alice, etc.—... No one has ever seen a "first-grade class," or a "fifth-grade class." What a teacher should see is a group of individuals, unique unto themselves. Not until differences are seen is the teacher ready to teach, because learning the child must precede teaching him.

EMMETT ALBERT BETTS, 1946

Questions to Ponder

1. If a parent approached me, would I be able to name a strength and a need of every child in my class?
2. Have I been treating every student fairly?

Opening Thoughts

A group of individuals, each unique unto themselves—these are our students. While we strive to treat each student fairly, fairness does not always mean giving the same treatment to every student. Some children learn to read with a highly structured phonics program while others benefit from a literature-based program. Some children may excel academically but require additional support due to emotional or physical needs. Teachers must address the uniqueness of every student and individualize instruction.

STUDENTS WITH SPECIAL NEEDS: YOUR ROLE IN THE IEP PROCESS

Since the 1975 passage of Public Law 94-142 (PL 94-142), the Education for All Handicapped Children Act, students with special needs have been included in our nation's classrooms. PL 94-142 brought new terms such as least restrictive environment, mainstreaming, and inclusion into educational vocabulary.

Today the Individuals with Disabilities Education Act (IDEA) protects the educational rights of individuals with special needs. Among those rights is the right to an Individualized Education Program (IEP). The IEP guarantees that educators, parents, and students will work together to make the school a welcoming and supportive environment for everyone with special needs.

General education teachers are part of the IEP team, which includes the student's parents, a special education teacher, a representative of the school district, and the student if the student is 16 years of age or older. Classroom teachers should be prepared to bring a portfolio of the student's classroom work and recent test data to discuss at the IEP meeting.

Inclusive practices bring the student with special needs into the general education classroom. In many cases a special education teacher enters the classroom to work with the general education teacher to provide services for the students with an IEP. When two teachers are able to combine their services in this manner, they share expertise, demonstrate teamwork, and bring effective instruction to all students.

Teamwork is essential when a general education teacher and a special education teacher work together to meet the needs of a group of students. Use the questions in Figure 8-1 to build an effective working relationship with a special education teacher.

Use the outline in Figure 8-2 to write lesson plans that include adaptations for students with special needs.

COLLABORATIVE TEACHING: GENERAL CLASSROOM TEACHERS AND SPECIAL EDUCATION TEACHERS WORKING TOGETHER

1. Why has _____ (student's name) been determined to be eligible for special education services?
2. How can I make my classroom a welcoming environment for this student?
3. What types of adaptations should I make to my lesson plans?
4. Is there assistive technology that would help this student?
5. What types of records should we keep to document progress as well as to diagnose strengths and needs?
6. You and I should meet frequently to monitor this student's progress. What is the best time for us to meet? Where should we meet?

FIGURE 8-1
An electronic version of this material can be found in Chapter 8 of the CD.

ADAPTIVE LESSON PLAN

Subject Area:

Grade/Age Level: Number of Students:

Lesson Title:

Time needed to complete this lesson:

Objective:

Standards:

Materials:

Procedure:

Adaptations:

Evaluation:

Reflection:

FIGURE 8-2
An electronic version of this material can be found in Chapter 8 of the CD.

CONSIDERATIONS FOR DIVERSE CLASSROOMS

Students respond well when their teachers show understanding for their strengths and needs. Simple acts of consideration can help students feel comfortable in the classroom and make it possible for them to learn in a supportive atmosphere.

Roll Call

A student once said, "Every year on the first day of school I dread the moment when the teacher calls the roll for the first time. My name is difficult to pronounce. Teachers read names such as John Green, Helen Brady, or Mary Baker easily but they pause and stumble a bit when they try to read my name. The hesitation in a teacher's voice makes me feel different and slightly unwelcome in the classroom."

It's hard to imagine that a routine task such as calling the roll could arouse insecurity in a student. This student's experience, however, reminds us that seemingly harmless acts can have negative effects on our students. When preparing for the first day of school, teachers should examine their class lists and ask members of the school community for help in pronouncing unfamiliar names.

Selecting Seats

When teaching math concepts, a new teacher asked her students to line up in the front of the room, from shortest to tallest. While the teacher felt that this activity reinforced the concepts of short and tall, some students were uncomfortable. The girl who towered over her classmates and the shortest boy in the class were embarrassed.

On the first day of school, a new teacher could allow the students to come into the room and select their own seats. By allowing the students to choose their own seats, the teacher can see where each student feels comfortable. (Some people prefer the first row and others like a middle seat!) When students follow classroom rules and complete their work efficiently, they should be permitted to select their own seats. Teachers can intervene and assign seats when they feel that a seating arrangement is detrimental to learning.

Speaking Clearly

A group of teachers assembled for a professional workshop. The speaker began by saying, "I don't like to use the microphone. Just raise your hand if you can't hear me." A participant with a hearing impairment raised her hand and corrected the speaker immediately. She said, "You have now forced me to call attention to my situation. Suppose I were a shy elementary or high school student in your class with a hearing impairment. My greatest wish might be to fit in with the other students. Your reluctance to use the microphone has now given me a dilemma. I must either raise my hand and ask for special treatment or sit through a class I cannot hear." This participant's comments remind us again of how seemingly benign remarks can cause anxiety for others. Teachers should not require students to make public statements concerning their special needs.

MEDIA ACCESS

Teachers often use digital video discs (DVDs), videotapes, films, and television programs to help students understand new concepts. Technology such as captioned programming for the hearing impaired and described programming for the visually impaired enable students with disabilities to enjoy programs with their classmates.

Captioned Programming

Captioned television programs, videotapes, and DVDs enable students with hearing impairments to enjoy programming with their classmates. In addition to assisting students with hearing impairments, captioned programming also offers benefits for students with average hearing ability. Repeated viewing of captioned programs can help students with poor word recognition skills build their sight vocabulary. Students who have difficulty comprehending a program often find that they gain greater understanding when they read the captions as they watch a program.

The Captioned Media Program, a federally funded program, lends open-captioned programs to teachers at no charge. When an open-captioned program is played on a standard video cassette recorder (VCR) or Digital Video Disc player (DVD), the captions appear without need of any special equipment. Users do not need to activate any special features on the VCR or DVD to make the captions appear.

To obtain open-captioned media, teachers should contact:

Website: http://www.cfv.org

Mailing Address: Captioned Media Program
National Association for the Deaf
1447 E. Main Street
Spartanburg, SC 29302

Telephone: 800-237-6213 (voice)
800-237-6819 (TTY)
800-538-5636 (FAX)

Described Programming

When a class is watching a film, a student with a visual impairment may listen to the film and glean what he can from the dialogue. That student, however, may hear sounds such as running footsteps and wonder which of the film's characters is running. Described programming provides narration that students with visual impairments can use to help them understand a film. When a film is described, visual elements such as scenery or a character's costume or gestures are described on a second audio track. Viewers can access this second audio track if they have a television, VCR, or DVDs, player with an SAP feature (Secondary Audio Program). If viewers do not have this equipment, they can purchase openly described videotapes or DVDs, which will enable them to hear these descriptions by using any VCR or DVD player.

Like captioned programming, described programming was developed to help individuals with disabilities. Educators are finding, however, that described programming can enhance comprehension for all students.

Information on described programming and distributors of described programming can be found by contacting Descriptive Video Service at WGBH, the Public Broadcasting Service station in Boston, MA.

Website: http://www.dvs.wgbh.org

Mailing Address: Descriptive Video Service
WGBH
125 Western Avenue
Boston, MA 02134

Telephone: 617-300-3600

E-mail: dvs@wgbh.org

Website: http://www.access.wgbh.org

Mailing Address: DVS Home Video
P.O. Box 55742
Indianapolis, IN 46205

Telephone: 1-317-579-0439

Audiobooks

Many students with learning disabilities have limited word recognition skills but strong listening comprehension ability. These students may have difficulty reading a textbook independently yet they are able to comprehend and participate in classroom discussions when the material is read to them. Teachers can assist these students by providing audio versions of classroom textbooks and trade books. The audio versions of trade books can often be found in retail stores and libraries. The private, non-profit organization—Recording for the Blind and Dyslexic (RFB&D)—offers audio versions of textbooks as well as related library services to individuals with print disabilities. They may be reached at:

Website: http://www.rfbd.org

Mailing Address: Recording for the Blind & Dyslexic
20 Roszel Road
Princeton, NJ 08540

Telephone: 1-800-221-4792

MY TEACHER SAID Anecdotes for Classroom Reflection and Discussion

There are exceptions to every rule and teachers must consider special circumstances when implementing policies. The following anecdote describes a situation that occurred when a teacher tried to rigidly

enforce a policy. Read and discuss the following tale with your colleagues. Did the teacher in this situation act appropriately?

No Hats Allowed

"Be firm and consistent," advised the principal, "If you make a rule, stick to it." Richard McCall, a new substitute teacher, followed this advice. Richard found himself in different classrooms each day and he took pride in enforcing basic rules such as requiring students to carry a hall pass when they left the classroom, asking students to always write their full names on their papers, and never allowing students to wear hats in the school building. Richard hoped that by enforcing school rules he would gain the respect of his principal and a permanent position in the school district.

One day the principal asked Richard to read announcements and introduce a guest speaker at a morning assembly. Richard waited on the stage as the classes took their seats in the auditorium. Suddenly Richard noticed a little girl with a scarf wrapped around her head. This was a clear violation of the school policy against wearing hats or head coverings during the school day. Richard stepped to the microphone. "I want the girl in the fifth row to take off that scarf immediately. You should know the rules. Students do not wear head scarves in this school." The room fell silent. Some people stared at the little girl with the scarf. Others looked at Richard, awaiting his next move. Then the little girl's teacher escorted her from her seat and walked out of the auditorium with her. Richard, feeling victorious in enforcing a policy, introduced the speaker and conducted the assembly with pride.

When the assembly was over, Richard walked quickly to the principal's office, expecting to be complimented on his effective management skills. "Did you know," said the principal, "that Beth has been having chemotherapy and she has been losing her hair? It is certainly important to enforce school rules, Richard. But was there another way to handle this situation?"

Questions

1. The principal said, "It is certainly important to enforce school rules. But was there another way to handle the situation?" How would you answer that question?
2. What could the principal and the teachers do to prevent situations like this in the future?
3. What could the substitute teacher learn from this situation?

Lingering Thoughts: A Time for Reflection

1. Have I been treating every student fairly?
2. How has discrimination impacted my personal and/or professional life? How has this caused me to react in the classroom?

References

Betts, E. (1946). *Foundations of reading instruction*. New York: American Book Company.

Chapter 9

ASSESSMENT AND RECORDKEEPING

Questions to Ponder

1. What steps can I take to develop an effective assessment plan for my students?
2. What is the most efficient way to file forms such as permission slips, book orders, and notes from parents?

Opening Thoughts

The passage of the No Child Left Behind (NCLB) Act of 2001 has heightened concerns for assessment and recordkeeping in the classroom. Most teachers are required to follow a standardized testing schedule described by NCLB guidelines. In addition to the NCLB high-stakes testing, teachers must also develop their own assessment procedures to determine their students' strengths and needs and to provide diagnostic instruction.

Assessments enable teachers to monitor progress, determine the effectiveness of their lessons, and make appropriate adjustments. Simple forms of assessments such as a collection of writing samples and rubrics for class projects can show a student's talents and offer guidance in planning new experiences.

WRITING SAMPLES

A consistent collection of writing samples helps teachers at every grade level measure progress. A writing sample shows the ways in which a student is able to organize his thoughts, summarize essential concepts, and use content area or descriptive vocabulary. Progress in using conventional spelling, punctuation,

KINDERGARTEN AND FIRST GRADE WRITING SAMPLE COLLECTION

My Name	Today's Date	My Sentence

FIGURE 9-1
An electronic version of this material can be found in Chapter 9 of the CD.

and handwriting or word processing skills can also be shown by a writing sample.

Children often show rapid growth in the primary grades and the brief form in Figure 9-1 can help teachers document progress and share milestones with their students' families.

Select one day every month on which you will ask each student to write his/her name and one sentence. Each month's entry should show improvement in letter formation. There should also be progress in spelling ability, punctuation, and sentence composition.

ELEMENTARY GRADES WRITING SAMPLE COLLECTION

Students can use the form in Figure 9-2 to record their written work and to develop portfolios. A portfolio is a collection of work students select to show their progress throughout the academic year. Each month the students should select one piece of writing they believe best shows their talents. The students should then use this form to list the name of their work and to comment on the work by stating why they selected that piece, what it means to them, or the inspiration for that piece. After the students have made their comments, the teacher should write responses to the students in the teacher comment column of the form.

WRITING LOG

Student's Name _____ Grade _____

Academic Year _____

Date	Title of Written Work	Student Comments	Teacher Comments

FIGURE 9-2
An electronic version of this material can be found in Chapter 9 of the CD.

RUBRICS

Science Fair Projects, Social Studies Dioramas, and Reader's Theatre Productions! There are many authentic ways for students to demonstrate that they have met standards and attained their educational goals. Teachers use authentic assessments to show that their students can apply skills and strategies to answer questions and solve problems in real-life situations.

Teachers develop rubrics so they can assign numerical grades to projects such as oral reports, posters, maps, and book reports. A rubric states the conditions that must be met and the potential grade a student can earn. Teachers develop assignment sheets and rubrics so that their students know their expectations and the manner in which they will be graded. The following example shows an assignment sheet and rubric for a fifth grade social studies project.

Sample Fifth Grade Social Studies Assignment Sheet and Rubric

Washington, D.C.: A Capital City

This month we will be learning about our nation's capital, Washington, D.C. We will be reading many books and magazines, watching and discussing films, and writing letters to our senators. As part of our study, you will have an opportunity to work with your classmates to prepare an oral report on an historic building or monument in Washington, D.C.

Your Assignment:

1. Find three students with whom you would like to work. Your group should select a building or monument from the list below.
   The White House
   The Capitol
   The National Cathedral
   The Lincoln Memorial
   The Washington Monument
   The Jefferson Memorial
   The Vietnam Veterans Memorial
   The Kennedy Center
2. Use the Internet as well as the books, magazines, and other print resources in our classroom to find pictures and learn more about the site you have chosen.
3. Make a poster illustrating and describing the site you have chosen.
4. Prepare a 3- to 5-minute oral presentation your group will give to the whole class. Every member of the group must participate in the oral presentation.
5. The following rubric distributed in class will be used to give your group a grade for this project. Use this rubric to help you plan your work.

RUBRIC FOR ORAL REPORT AND POSTER
HISTORIC BUILDINGS AND MONUMENTS IN WASHINGTON, D.C.

	Possible Points	Points for Your Group
Did the group members give significant information in the oral report? Was the report accurate?	30	
Were the group members able to answer questions from the audience?	15	
Did all members of the group participate?	10	
Did the group members speak clearly?	10	
Did the group follow the 3- to 5-minute time requirement?	10	
Did the group prepare a poster that gave significant information?	20	
Was the poster legible and free from spelling or punctuation errors?	5	
Total Points	100	

KEEPING RECORDS

Before you assign homework or plan a field trip, develop a system for keeping records and dealing with the paperwork that can accumulate. Organize the drawers in your classroom filing cabinet so that you are prepared to file materials such as permission slips, letters from parents, school policy sheets, and assessments. Purchase a three-ring binder and devote a section to each class that you teach. As you develop forms throughout the school year, put a blank copy of each form in the appropriate section of your binder. If you file these forms carefully, you'll have less work to do next year.

STUDENT CONTACT INFORMATION

Student Name	Parent/ Guardian Name	Home Telephone	Cell Phone or Additional Phone	E-mail Address

FIGURE 9-3
An electronic version of this material can be found in Chapter 9 of the CD.

Make several copies of the chart in Figure 9-3.

1. Keep a copy in your desk at school.
2. Keep a copy in your home.
3. Place one copy in a folder for anyone who may be substituting in your classroom.
4. Give a copy to the school nurse.
5. Give a copy to your school administrator.

Remember: **This information should not be posted in an area of public access.**

READING LOGS

Organization is the key to success in most endeavors. The reading logs included in this chapter (Figures 9-4 through 9-7) will help your students organize information, track their progress, and share comments on their reading.

Four reading logs are provided so that teachers can select the logs that are most appropriate for their classrooms.

LOG 1—STUDENT READING LOG

After we read a book, memories of special characters and places linger in our minds. Use this reading log to help you remember all of the books you read.

Write the book's title and author on the chart. Then write the date on which you finished reading this book. Give your comments on the book. What part did you like the best? Is this a book that you will want to read again? Give the book a rating from 1 to 5. A rating of 5 is the highest recommendation. If you give a book a rating of 4 or 5, that means that you truly enjoyed the book and you think that others might also like it. A rating of 1 to 2 indicates that you did not enjoy this book and do not recommend it to others.

Title	Author	Date I read this book	My comments on this book	Rating

FIGURE 9-4
An electronic version of this material can be found in Chapter 9 of the CD.

Log 1

Log 1 (Figure 9-4) has spaces for students to record titles and authors as well as the dates on which they read various texts. The fourth column provides space for the students to write a comment related to the text they read. Students are asked to use the final column to rate the text.

Log 2

Log 2 (Figure 9-5) has a space for students to record a date and the pages or text that they read on that date. In the third column students can write a comment related to the text they read.

LOG 2 – READING LOG

Student Name _____

Date	Text or Pages Read	My comments about my reading . . .

FIGURE 9-5
An electronic version of this material can be found in Chapter 9 of the CD.

LOG 3—READING LOG

Student Name _____

Date	Text or Pages Read	My comments about my reading . . .	Teacher Comments

FIGURE 9-6
An electronic version of this material can be found in Chapter 9 of the CD.

LOG 4—READING LOG

Student Name _____

Date	Text or Pages Read	Adult Signature	My comments about my reading . . .	Teacher Comments

FIGURE 9-7
An electronic version of this material can be found in Chapter 9 of the CD.

Log 3

Log 3 (Figure 9-6) has a space for students to record a date and the pages or text that they read on that date. In the third column students can write a comment related to the text they read. The fourth column provides a space for the teacher to give a comment in reply.

Log 4

Log 4 (Figure 9-7) can be used to record homework assignments. There are columns for students to record the date, the pages they read, and their comments on the reading. There is also a place for an adult signature to verify that a student completed the home reading assignment and a place for the teacher to respond to the student.

MY TEACHER SAID Anecdotes for Classroom Reflection and Discussion

Parents have needs and concerns that teachers must address in a professional and ethical manner. The following anecdote describes the way in which a teacher responded to a parent's request. Read and discuss this tale with your colleagues. Did the teacher in this situation act appropriately?

The Brightest in the Class

Six-year-old Joey Henderson and his mother entered the classroom to greet Gloria Brady, Joey's new teacher. "Joey will be your biggest problem," said Mrs. Henderson. "Joey is so bright that it's hard to keep him busy and challenged. The work you give your other students will be too easy for Joey."

"It's nice to meet you and Joey," said Gloria. "I strive to find the right level of work for every student. It's a bit like the story of Goldilocks and the Three Bears. Some work is too hard, some work is too easy and then there is work that is just right. I try to find that *just right* level for every student."

Throughout the next few weeks, Mrs. Henderson visited the school periodically. She stopped by the classroom to chat when she brought Joey to school each morning. She examined Joey's papers when she picked him up after school.

One Friday afternoon, Mrs. Henderson requested a conference with the teacher. She began by saying, "Joey told me that you put him in a guided reading group with five other children, Eileen, Tony, Therese, Dave, and Carleene. Those children live near my home and I have known them for a long time. I know that they don't read as well as Joey. They will hold Joey back. We'll have to place Joey in a more advanced group."

"I appreciate your concern," said Miss Brady, "but I considered many factors as I was organizing the guided reading groups. This group of children is working well together and everyone is learning. Please remember also that these groups are temporary. Our guided reading groups change frequently during the school year."

"But those children are holding Joey back now. He is too bright to be working with them and he can't wait until it's time for you to change your groups. I honestly don't think that there are any children in this class who can keep up with Joey. Perhaps we should consider moving him to another class or the next grade."

"Mrs. Henderson," said the teacher, "Joey has been placed correctly and everyone in this school is working hard to give him appropriate instruction." "I don't agree," said Mrs. Henderson and she left the school.

When Monday came, Gloria entered the school with dread. Just as she predicted, Mrs. Henderson was waiting for her at the classroom door. "Good news," said Mrs. Henderson. "I have the information we need to make our decision on Joey's placement. I know that you are extremely busy teaching every day and you don't have time to make detailed assessments of every student. My good friend Grace, however, is a reading specialist. I asked her to come to Joey's birthday party on Saturday and test the children who are in Joey's guided reading group. While the children played games at the party, Grace quickly tested them and found their true reading levels. She confirmed my suspicions. Joey is reading much better than everyone else. I brought the scores for Eileen, Tony, Therese, Dave, and Carleene so that you can compare their scores to Joey's scores."

Mrs. Henderson gave Gloria a stack of papers but Gloria quickly gave them back. "I don't think I should read these," said Gloria. "This is confidential information. I'd like you to speak with our principal, Mrs. Quinn." "But you and I must schedule a conference to determine the right placement for Joey," said Mrs. Henderson. "No, we must meet with Mrs. Quinn," said Gloria, "We can't have a conference unless our principal is present."

Gloria discussed the events with her principal and scheduled a conference at a time when she, the parent, and the principal could attend.

Questions

1. How do you think the principal will react to this situation?
2. What would you have done if you were this teacher? Should the teacher have examined the scores and discussed them with the parent?
3. Did the outside reading specialist act in a professional and ethical manner?
4. Suppose individualized testing showed that the student, Joey, was actually reading significantly above grade level. Could a teacher meet his needs in a traditional classroom?

Lingering Thoughts: A Time for Reflection

1. Am I dealing with paperwork satisfactorily or am I drowning in forms and records? How can I deal with paperwork more efficiently?
2. Have I developed a system to monitor the progress of my students? How can I improve my assessment program?

Chapter 10

CERTIFICATION AND PROFESSIONAL DEVELOPMENT

Questions to Ponder

1. I have worked hard to become a teacher. What steps can I take to continue to improve my teaching?
2. How can I use my skills outside the classroom? Are there alternative career opportunities for individuals with a degree in education?

Opening Thoughts

Certification and professional development can lead to personal satisfaction as well as career opportunities. While most teachers find employment in traditional settings, new positions are emerging for certified teachers. The growth of charter schools, tutoring services, online schools, and educational publishing have created additional venues for teachers to apply their talents. After completing certification requirements, new teachers can learn of developments and investigate employment opportunities by joining professional organizations, attending conferences, and reading professional literature. (A directory of professional organizations as well as a directory of periodicals in education can be found in the Resources section of this text and on the accompanying CD.)

CERTIFICATION

Certification regulations guarantee that every child will have a teacher who can create an effective and safe learning environment. Upon successful completion of coursework, individuals wishing to become teachers receive their degrees from an accredited college or university. Teaching certificates are issued by a state department of education, not by the college or university. Each state determines its own requirements and candidates should visit a state department of education's website to learn the requirements for the state in which they wish to teach.

CHAPTER 10 Certification and Professional Development

The Council of Chief State School Officers (CCSSO) maintains a website to help prospective teachers find certification requirements for each state, the District of Columbia, the Department of Defense Activity, and five extra state jurisdictions. This nonpartisan, nonprofit organization leads efforts to maintain quality in the preparation, licensure, and professional development of teachers.

The Council of Chief State School Officers (CCSSO) can be reached at:

Website: http://www.ccsso.org

Mailing Address: Council of Chief State School Officers
One Massachusetts Avenue NW, Suite 700
Washington, DC 20001-1431

Telephone: 202-336-7000

Fax: 202-408-8072

The PRAXIS Series: Assessments for Certification

As part of the certification process, many states require candidates to pass written examinations. Some states have created their own assessment instruments while others use the PRAXIS Series: Professional Assessments for Beginning Teachers, administered by ETS, the Educational Testing Service, based in Princeton, New Jersey.

The PRAXIS Series is divided into three categories. PRAXIS I assessments measure basic academic skills such as mathematics, reading, and writing. Designed for individuals entering a teacher-training program, students at many colleges take the PRAXIS I assessments during their freshman or sophomore year of study. Graduate students may be required to take PRAXIS I assessments as part of the admission process to a teacher preparation program.

PRAXIS II assessments measure the subject matter knowledge and understanding of instructional techniques that beginning teachers need to find success in the classroom. PRAXIS II tests are often taken by students in their senior or final year of a teacher preparation program. Teachers in the first years of their career may use the PRAXIS III, classroom performance assessments, as part of their state's certification process. There are many instruments within the PRAXIS series and candidates for teacher certification must contact their state department of education to determine which PRAXIS assessments their state requires as well as the scores needed to meet certification requirements for that state. Information regarding registration for the PRAXIS series can be obtained by contacting the Educational Testing Service at:

Website: http://www.ets.org/praxis/index.html

Mailing Address: Educational Testing Service
Rosedale Road
Princeton, NJ 08541

Telephone: 609-921-9000

Fax: 609-734-5410

Maintaining Certification

Novice teachers are usually able to work for a brief period of time with an initial certificate. Most states then require teachers to complete an induction program, graduate coursework, and/or a period of classroom observation to maintain certification. Regulations vary for each state and teachers should continually check their state website to make certain that they are following the current guidelines.

National Board Certification

Certification by a state department of education is a minimum requirement for individuals wishing to attain a teaching position. Teachers who wish to extend their training and commitment beyond the minimum requirements may also seek National Board Certification.

The National Board for Professional Teaching Standards (NBPTS) was founded to create standards and performance-based assessments that enable teachers to demonstrate mastery of the standards. Teachers with a baccalaureate degree and three years of classroom experience in a public or private school are eligible for National Board Certification. The voluntary process asks teachers to submit documents such as teaching portfolios, student work samples, and videotapes of their work in the classroom. Candidates are required to complete written exercises that assess their subject matter knowledge and understanding of educational theory and techniques. Upon completion of the program, certification is granted for ten years. After the ten-year period, teachers must apply for renewal to maintain their National Board Certification. National Board Certification is a rigorous process that requires commitment and tremendous skill. It is a worthy goal that provides professional development and helps a teacher to earn the respect of his/her colleagues.

The National Board for Professional Teaching Standards can be reached at:

Website: http://www.nbpts.org

Mailing Address: National Board for Professional Teaching Standards
1525 Wilson Blvd, Suite 500
Arlington, VA 22209

Telephone: 703-465-2700

SUBSTITUTE TEACHING

Individuals may become substitute teachers to earn income while they are seeking a permanent position, awaiting a move to a new area, or meeting family obligations. Substitute teaching can serve as an introduction to the classroom for those considering a career change or for college students pursuing a degree in education. By teaching in a variety of schools, substitute teachers grow professionally as they face the challenges of diverse classrooms.

The requirements for substitute teaching vary from state to state. Most states require substitute teachers to have the same credentials as members of the full-time, permanent faculty. In areas where there is a shortage of certified teachers, however, individuals may be permitted to work for a limited time as a substitute teacher without certification or a degree in education. In parts of New Jersey, for example, individuals who possess a minimum of 60 credits from an accredited college can be issued a county substitute certificate for per diem substitute teaching (N.J.A.C. 6:11-4.5). To become a substitute teacher, individuals should contact a school district's personnel office to learn their hiring practices and policies. Some districts interview substitute teaching candidates and then call these individuals when they are needed. Other districts engage the services of private employment agencies to interview substitute teaching candidates and to provide substitute teachers on an as-needed basis.

Pros and Cons of Substitute Teaching

Pros	Cons
You will have an opportunity to meet many educators and gain a broad perspective on teaching.	You will not have an opportunity to develop long-term relationships with colleagues or students.
At the end of the day you will walk out of the school with no lingering responsibilities. You won't spend evenings and weekends grading papers, preparing report cards, or writing reports.	You will not be able to develop and implement long-term projects such as thematic units, class plays, or research assignments.
You will have the flexibility to meet family obligations, take vacations, or pursue recreational interests without the constraints of a full-time teaching position.	You will face the insecurity of never knowing when or where you might be asked to teach.
You will have a variety of experiences that will teach you a great deal about the profession.	You may not be able to participate in workshops and professional development programs that are offered to the permanent faculty.
In some states, individuals are permitted to work as substitute teachers without	In many states, college graduates are required to teach for a specific number of years

passing the PRAXIS examinations, which are required of permanent faculty members.	in order to gain permanent certification. Per diem substitute teaching is usually not credited toward the required time.
You will interact with a large number of students.	You will not have the fulfillment that comes from nurturing students throughout a school year.
Substitute teaching offers an opportunity to work periodically and gain extra income.	Substitute teachers usually have less access to health insurance and other financial benefits.

When the Phone Rings: Being Prepared

Substitute teachers usually receive early morning phone calls or e-mail messages summoning them to a school with little notice. If you plan to substitute, be prepared by having a tote bag packed with supplies to help you and your students have a smooth, productive experience. Fill your bag with the materials suggested here.

- ◆ **Dry Erase Markers/Chalk**
  Although schools usually have these supplies, some substitute teachers have found themselves in classrooms with no chalk and dry erase markers that are old and fading. It's hard to spend the day effectively when the students cannot see the material you are writing on the whiteboard or when they cannot write on the board themselves. Be prepared by bringing your own chalk and dry erase markers to ensure a more productive day for all.

- ◆ **Newspapers**
  Keep a selection of newspapers, including the colorful Sunday comic strips, in your tote bag. Read aloud articles of national and international events to engage the students in discussion. You can use newspapers to create math lessons with weather charts, stock market reports, and classified advertisements. The comic strips can be used for sequencing activities, art projects, and creative writing.

- ◆ **Read-Aloud Selections**
  You may wish to read aloud to a class when they have finished their work or when they are awaiting a summons to the lunchroom or auditorium. Have a book of short stories in your tote bag so that you are always prepared with a good tale. Suggested titles include *The Book of Virtues for Young People* edited by William J. Bennett and *Five-Minute Mini-Mysteries* by Stan Smith.
  The Book of Virtues for Young People
  Edited by William J. Bennett
  With this collection of short stories, folktales, and poems in your bag, you will always be able to find a selection to fit the moment.

Five-Minute Mini-Mysteries
   by Stan Smith
   Author Stan Smith has created a series of five-minute mini-mysteries, which students love to solve. Each mystery is approximately four pages long and the reader is given several clues to solve the puzzle. The solutions are given in the back of the book. By reading these mysteries aloud, a substitute teacher can help students develop listening comprehension and can engage the students in lively discussions.

Engaging Activities

While most teachers will leave lesson plans for a substitute teacher, it is wise to be prepared with activities that could be adapted to meet the strengths and needs of students of various ages. On the following pages you will find activities for the primary grades using a quilting theme and activities for the upper elementary grades using newspapers to engage students and develop skills.

The Patchwork Quilt: Sewing Together Activities for Literacy, Mathematics, and Art

The art of quilting can inspire a day's worth of meaningful activities that build skills in literacy, mathematics, and art.

Literacy

Read *The Patchwork Quilt* by Valerie Flournoy to the class. This beautiful picture book shows the ways in which a group can work together to create a quilt that holds memories. As you read the book aloud, stop periodically to ask the students to make predictions and to discuss the relationships between the characters.

After you have read and discussed the text, ask the students to write a reflection upon the story.

Mathematics

Quilters must add and subtract as well as measure precisely to complete projects. Give your students quilt-related mathematical problems such as the following:

1. Dawn made a quilt for her new baby sister. There were nine squares on the quilt. If it took Dawn three hours to make one square, how long did it take her to make the entire quilt?

2. Tara picked up her scissors and cut out small hearts to place on a new quilt that she was making. There would be nine squares on her quilt and Tara wanted to have two hearts on each square. How many hearts would Tara need?

3. John wanted to buy fabric to make a quilt. The fabric cost $3.00 per yard and John needed four yards to make the quilt. How much money would John need to buy four yards of fabric?

Art

When you are a substitute teacher, you may not have time to make a fabric quilt with a class. You can, however, make paper quilts with the students by using construction paper or wallpaper samples.

You could give the students squares of white paper and ask them to draw a picture on a particular theme. The squares could then be assembled to form a quilt on a bulletin board. If you wish to give the students practice in measuring and cutting, you could distribute construction paper or wallpaper samples and ask the children to cut and assemble pieces for quilt squares.

Newspaper Notes: Reading, Writing, Arithmetic

Carry a newspaper in your emergency substitute teaching tote and you will always have a handy source for lesson ideas.

Literacy

Select newspaper articles that match the developmental stage and interests of your students. Stories of local high school athletes, for example, often become motivating reading material for elementary students. Read and discuss the articles with your students. Provide time for the students to write a response and share their written response with classmates.

Mathematics

There are many ways to use the newspaper to build math skills. Suggested activities:

- **What's the Weather?**
    Help students use the newspaper weather section to calculate the difference in temperature between two cities.

- **Supermarket Savvy**
    Use grocery store circulars and coupons to help students calculate the cost of a family meal.

- **Estimation**
    Ask students to estimate the cost of purchases such as a used car, musical instrument, or furniture. After the students have made their estimates, ask them to use the classified section of the newspaper to determine the accuracy of their estimations.

Social Studies

Introduce the terms local, national, and international by selecting and reading articles from the newspaper. Read brief articles aloud and help the children to classify the articles as local, national, or international. If a map is available, ask the children to use the map to locate the setting of the article.

THE SUBSTITUTE'S SUMMARY

Hello!

I recently had an opportunity to work with your students. I placed notes the students brought from home and samples of the work they completed in the folder that accompanies this note.

My best moment with your students came when:
_____
_____
_____

We completed the following:
_____
_____
_____

If you have any questions about our work, you can reach me at _____.

Best wishes,

_____

FIGURE 10-1
An electronic version of this material can be found in Chapter 10 of the CD.

The Substitute's Summary

When you have completed an assignment as a substitute teacher, leave a note (Figure 10-1) to let the permanent teacher know what transpired during his/her absence. By letting the permanent teacher know the material you covered and the responses of the students, you will ensure continuity in the students' educational program.

PROFESSIONAL DEVELOPMENT

You studied for many years to earn a teaching certificate. This certificate demonstrates that you have the knowledge and skills to lead a class and to communicate effectively with students, parents, and colleagues. Education is a dynamic profession, however, and research brings new instructional techniques to the classroom. Legislation changes the ways in which we assess and report student learning. It is vital, therefore, that teachers become lifelong learners, open to new ideas and committed to regularly scheduled maintenance of their teaching skills.

Professional development for teachers can take many forms. Often teachers in private and public schools are required to attend sessions in their buildings to learn of new assessment techniques, curriculum revisions, or classroom management techniques. Large school districts may offer regional workshops for their teachers. Some districts reimburse teachers who attend conferences or graduate classes away from the school building. When offered a position at a public or private school, it is appropriate for the job candidate to ask the interviewer to describe the professional development opportunities associated with that position. This question shows the interviewer that the candidate recognizes the need to regularly update his/her skills and to provide the students of that school with the most current, effective instruction.

A Word Wall for Teachers

There's a word wall in your classroom. The word wall helps your students spell words they need to complete written assignments. It reminds them of descriptive words that can enhance their writing.

Consider making your own Teacher's Word Wall, or discreetly hidden word list, to guide your professional writing. A Teacher's Word Wall can assist you in writing reports and anecdotal records. It can save you from the embarrassment of misspelling or using educational terms incorrectly.

Common errors for teachers to avoid include:

Reading Aloud

This term is preferable to the term *reading out loud*.

Children or Students, Not Kids

The young people we meet in the classroom should be addressed as children or students in formal reports.

Sight Words, Not Cite Words

Sight words are words that a student should recognize immediately. Cite words would be an incorrect term for this concept.

Primer and Preprimer, Not Premier

An early reading level is called a *primer*. *Premier* refers to an opening night.

Refer to the textbooks you used in college and graduate school to find professional vocabulary and begin building your Teacher's Word Wall. Timely use of the Teacher's Word Wall can improve your image in the minds of supervisors, colleagues, and parents.

BOOK CLUBS FOR TEACHERS

What are you reading? We ask our students that question and we encourage them to read to expand their vocabulary and awareness of other viewpoints and cultures. Often we provide opportunities for our students to participate in literature circles or book clubs so that they can read and discuss intriguing books with their peers.

Many teachers find that they can experience similar rewards when they participate in book clubs with their fellow educators. Teaching can be a tiring and lonely experience. While each day brings rewards, there are also conflicts and challenges. Teachers can relieve stress and form bonds by establishing book clubs with their peers. Teachers' Book Clubs give student teachers, novice teachers, and veteran teachers common ground to discuss social issues, history, or current events. Book clubs provide an opportunity for teachers to meet informally to share their views on topics other than the curriculum, school schedule, or individual student needs.

If your school has a Teachers' Book Club, consider joining so that you can talk regularly with your new colleagues. Membership in the book club may help you establish friendships and appreciate the special gifts and insights of teachers throughout your building. If your school does not have a Teachers' Book Club, start one! By establishing a Teachers' Book Club, you will demonstrate that you have the initiative to be a positive, contributing member of the school community.

Organizing a Teachers' Book Club

Begin by defining the purpose for your Teachers' Book Club. Some Teachers' Book Clubs serve as a forum for professional development in which teachers read and discuss books on topics such as curriculum trends, instructional methodology, or research in education. Other teachers become familiar with new titles for children and young adults by discussing the books that their students are reading. For example, middle school teachers might read and discuss novels written for students in grades four to eight. High school teachers could discuss books on their students' required reading lists. Many Teachers' Book Clubs meet purely to enjoy good literature. They read fiction and nonfiction found on lists of best-selling books or recommended by friends. Consider the purpose and the types of books you would like to read before inviting other teachers to join your book club. Establishing a purpose will help your group decide which books they would like to read.

After establishing your purpose, survey the teachers in your school to determine the best time and place for the book club to meet. Some Teachers' Book Clubs have early morning breakfast meetings while others prefer an afternoon social at the end of the school day. Sometimes teachers would rather have an evening or weekend meeting at a setting away from the school. A weekend meeting at a restaurant or a member's home can transform a Teachers' Book Club meeting into a much anticipated social event.

Suggested Book Club Titles

I. Books for Professional Development

Knowing How: Researching and Writing Nonfiction 3-8

McMackin, M., & Siegel, B. (2002). *Knowing How: Researching and Writing Nonfiction 3-8*. Portland, Maine: Stenhouse Publishers.

> How can one teacher supervise 25 fifth grade students as they research and write individualized reports? In *Knowing How*, veteran teacher Barbara Siegel and Lesley University professor Mary McMackin show that with organization and knowledge of the writing process, teachers and students can engage in meaningful research and writing projects. *Knowing How* gives practical advice that can help teachers build a writing community in their classrooms.

Marva Collins' Way

Collins, M., & Tamarkin, C. (1982). *Marva Collins' Way*. Los Angeles: J. P. Tarcher, Inc.

> Frustrated with the daily struggles she faced in the Chicago Public Schools, veteran educator Marva Collins opened her own school to show that high expectations and a demanding curriculum could empower children. *Marva Collins' Way* is the story of one teacher's faith in her convictions and the community and children she served.

No One to Play With: The Social Side of Learning Disabilities

Osman, B. (in association with Blinder, H.) (1982). *No One to Play With: The Social Side of Learning Disabilities*. Novato, CA: Academic Therapy Publications.

> Betty Osman, Ph.D., is a psychologist who understands the frustrations of children and adults with learning disabilities. In *No One to Play With*, Osman shows that the effects of learning disabilities are not limited to the classroom. Her book will help teachers understand the ways in which they can support every student's quest for academic and social success.

The Read-Aloud Handbook, 5th Edition

Trelease, J. (2001). *The Read-Aloud Handbook* (5th ed.). New York: Penguin Books.

> Jim Trelease reminds us of the importance of the oral tradition and the benefits of reading aloud. This text contains anecdotes on reading aloud, the stages of read-aloud, read-aloud success stories, and a treasury of read-alouds. *The Read-Aloud Handbook* will inspire teachers to visit the library to get great books to share with their classes.

Trading Cards to Comic Strips: Popular Culture Texts and Literacy Learning in Grades K-8

Xu, S. H., with Perkins, R. S., & Zunich, L. O. (2005). *Trading Cards to Comic Strips: Popular Culture Texts and Literacy Learning in Grades K-8*. Newark, DE: International Reading Association.

> When films, television programs, or comic books excite students, wise teachers capitalize upon their interest to build skills. This text contains ideas for linking standards-based literacy instruction to popular culture texts. *Trading Cards to Comic Strips: Popular Culture Texts and Literacy Learning in Grades K-8* combines theory with practice by offering research as well as sample letters to parents/guardians, lists of websites, and reproducibles to use in the classroom.

Ways of Writing with Young Kids

Edwards, S. A., Maloy, R. W., & Verock-O'Loughlin, R. E. (2003). *Ways of Writing with Young Kids*. Boston: Allyn and Bacon.

Ways of Writing with Young Kids (WOW) helps teachers bring a positive, inspiring focus to writing with students in kindergarten to grade three. There are examples, guides, and practical tips to motivate teachers and students.

II. Books for Inspiration

Thank You, Mr. Falker

Polacco, Patricia. (1998). *Thank You, Mr. Falker*. New York: Philomel Books.

When you feel that you aren't making a difference in the classroom, read *Thank You, Mr. Falker* by Patricia Polacco. *Thank You, Mr. Falker* tells the story of a little girl's struggle with a learning disability and the sensitive teacher who helped her read and believe in herself. This beautiful picture book has messages for the elementary students who may hear it as a read-aloud and for the teachers who have the privilege of reading it with them.

Oh the Places You'll Go

Seuss, T. G. (1990). *Oh the Places You'll Go*. New York: Random House.

You enjoyed the nonsense and rhyme of Dr. Seuss when you were in kindergarten. Now Dr. Seuss has words of encouragement for you as you begin your career as a teacher. *Oh the Places You'll Go* is Dr. Seuss's gift to young adults to inspire them to do their best for the children who will be reading his books.

My Teacher Rides a Harley: Enhancing K–5 Literacy through Songwriting

Dulabaum, G. (2003). *My Teacher Rides a Harley: Enhancing K–5 Literacy through Songwriting*. Gainesville, FL: Maupin House Publishing.

My Teacher Rides a Harley: Enhancing K–5 Literacy through Songwriting offers entertaining poetry and songs for a variety of school-related occasions. The book comes with an accompanying CD of songs that will boost spirits at the end of a long teaching day.

III. Fiction and Nonfiction for Teachers' Book Clubs

Among Schoolchildren

Kidder, T. (1989). *Among Schoolchildren*. Boston: Houghton Mifflin Company.

Teachers reading *Among Schoolchildren* will find themselves in these pages. *Among Schoolchildren* chronicles the daily challenges and triumphs faced by a fifth grade teacher and student teacher. The manner in which these educators interact with colleagues and students will offer guidance and optimism to novice teachers.

The Five People You Meet in Heaven

Albom, M. (2003). *The Five People You Meet in Heaven*. New York: Hyperion.

The Five People You Meet in Heaven shows that the world is truly a very small place and all of our lives are interconnected. It offers inspirational reading for book club members.

A Hope in the Unseen: An American Odyssey from the Inner City to the Ivy League

Suskind, R. (1998). *A Hope in the Unseen: An American Odyssey from the Inner City to the Ivy League*. New York: Broadway.

> *A Hope in the Unseen: An American Odyssey from the Inner City to the Ivy League* is the inspiring true story of Cedric Jennings's journey from a troubled Washington, D.C. high school to Brown University. Cedric's struggle to find academic success will raise many questions for students and teachers.

Profiles in Courage for Our Time

Kennedy, C. (ed.). (2002). *Profiles in Courage for Our Time*. New York: Hyperion Press.

> *Profiles in Courage for Our Time* is a collection of essays honoring men and women who risked their careers by voicing unpopular opinions. Not all book club members will agree that the subjects profiled acted selflessly or that their acts were truly laudable. Book club selections should raise questions, however, and a discussion on this book will bring many divergent opinions to the forefront.

The Right to Privacy

Alderman, E., & Kennedy, C. (1995). *The Right to Privacy*. New York: Alfred A. Knopf.

> In *The Right to Privacy*, authors Ellen Alderman and Caroline Kennedy take complicated laws and show how those laws affect the privacy of every citizen.

Tisha

Specht, R. (1976). *Tisha*. New York: St. Martins Press.

> *Tisha* tells the true story of 19-year-old Anne Hobbs who traveled to the remote town of Chicken, Alaska, in 1927 to teach in a one-room school. Teachers today will marvel at Anne's inventiveness and the perseverance she showed in handling surprises from the climate, her students, and the townspeople.

Tuesdays with Morrie

Albom, M. (1997). *Tuesdays with Morrie*. Rockland, MA: Wheeler Publishing, Inc.

> A Tuesday spent with Morrie can change your perspective on life, death, and the relationships that develop along the journey. In *Tuesdays with Morrie* author Mitch Albom shares conversations he had with his college professor, Morrie Schwartz, as Schwartz faced approaching death from amyotrophic lateral sclerosis (ALS), Lou Gehrig's disease. This text raises intriguing questions that can ignite book club discussions.

IV. Chapter Books for Elementary Teachers

Teachers of students in the upper grades may enjoy reading and discussing these chapter books with colleagues to identify themes and plan thematic units.

Crash

Spinelli, J. (1996). *Crash*. New York: Random House.

> Newbery Award-winning author Jerry Spinelli has a unique talent for capturing the hopes and fears of students. His novel, *Crash*, offers many lessons on the effects of bullying, the power of compassion, and respect for the elderly.

Esperanza Rising

Ryan, P. M. (2000). *Esperanza Rising.* New York: Scholastic.

> Born into a life of wealth and privilege, 13-year-old Esperanza triumphs over adversity when crime strikes her family. This historical fiction selection traces Esperanza's journey from Mexico to California during the Great Depression. The text offers history lessons as well as lessons in coping with life's surprises.

Frindle

Clements, A. (1996). *Frindle.* New York: Simon & Schuster.

> Fifth grade student Nick tries to distract his language arts teacher, Mrs. Granger, by asking her how new words get into the dictionary. When the teacher replies that ordinary people can coin new words, Nick decides to annoy and challenge Mrs. Granger by inventing a new word for pen, frindle. Nick's insistence upon using this word leads to humorous situations and appearances on late night talk shows.
>
> *Frindle* shows the difficulty that can result when teachers and students are unable to communicate. Teachers' Book Clubs can use *Frindle* as a basis for interesting discussions on the rights of teachers and students.

The Giver

Lowry, L. (1993). *The Giver.* New York: Bantam Doubleday Dell Books for Young Readers.

> *The Giver* is a disturbing book of life in a futuristic society. In this society, citizens are relieved of the burden of choice. Everything from an individual's daily diet to his occupation is regulated by the elders of the society. *The Giver* can spark many fascinating discussions between students and their teachers. *The Giver* is part of a trilogy by Newbery Award winner, Lois Lowry, which includes *Gathering Blue* (2000) and *The Messenger* (2004).

Stone Fox

Gardiner, J. R. (1980). *Stone Fox.* New York: Harper Collins Publishers.

> *Stone Fox* tells the story of 10-year-old Willy who tried to save his grandfather's farm by winning cash in a dogsled race. This story of perseverance and compassion can inspire students and teachers.

Touching Spirit Bear

Mikaelsen, B. (2001). *Touching Spirit Bear.* New York: Harper Collins Publishers.

> Fifteen-year-old Cole Matthews has been convicted of a serious crime. Instead of receiving a jail sentence, however, a judge allows Cole to participate in a Native American Rehabilitation Program. Cole's journey through the rehabilitation program and the truths he learns can be enlightening for older students. Members of a Teachers' Book Club will find much to discuss as they read and consider the ways in which they could use this book in their classrooms.

Choices Booklist: Great Books to Share With Students

When you moved into your new classroom, you brought boxes of your favorite books to share with your students. Your Babysitters' Club books, Goosebumps, and A to Z Mysteries have been unpacked and are waiting on the shelves for eager readers. While it is fun to share your personal favorites, teachers also need to be aware of new trends and titles. The International Reading Association (IRA) conducts a yearly poll of students, teachers, and librarians to find the best new books for children and young adults. Each of their three Choices lists (Children's Choices, Teachers' Choices, and Young Adults' Choices) can be found by visiting the website for the International Reading Association (IRA) at: http://www.reading.org.

- **Children's Choices**
  Books found on the Children's Choices list are appropriate for students in kindergarten through grade six. Each of the 100 books appearing on this annual list has been recommended by children. The Children's Choices list is published in the IRA journal, *The Reading Teacher*, every October.

- **Teachers' Choices**
  The annual Teachers' Choices list provides reviews of recently published books, which could make outstanding contributions to the curriculum. Each year the Teachers' Choices list is published in the November issue of the IRA journal, *The Reading Teacher*.

- **Young Adults' Choices**
  Books found on the Young Adults' Choices list are appropriate for grades six and older. The books appearing on this list have been selected and reviewed by teams of teenagers. Every year the Young Adults' Choices list is published in the November issue of the IRA publication, *The Journal of Adolescent & Adult Literacy*.

OPPORTUNITIES BEYOND THE CLASSROOM

Although you have prepared for a career in the classroom, the skills you have acquired in a teacher education program can give you access to professional opportunities beyond the schoolhouse doors. Certified teachers can find financially and professionally rewarding full- and part-time employment with tutoring centers, educational publishers, and community organizations.

Tutoring

Throughout the years, many teachers have turned to tutoring for supplemental income. Those wishing to work independently may begin by scanning the employment section of the local newspaper to learn appropriate rates for their area. Independent tutors often find that they can use meeting rooms in public libraries or community buildings to see clients. Some teachers prefer to serve as employees of large-scale tutoring programs such as the Sylvan Learning Centers or Huntington Learning Centers. These centers can offer flexible hours and freedom from the recordkeeping necessary for independent tutors.

Educational Publishing

Publishers of curriculum materials such as textbooks, software, and manipulative materials offer a variety of employment opportunities for trained teachers. Teachers are needed in the sales force to present new products to school district administrators and to demonstrate instructional materials during professional development workshops. There is also a need for creative teachers to work with educational publishers to develop new classroom materials. Teachers can find employment opportunities by visiting the websites of their favorite educational publishers.

Field Testing Opportunities

Publishers of standardized assessments such as the Woodcock Reading Mastery Tests-Revised or the Peabody Picture Vocabulary Test often need teachers to field test their materials. Field testers administer new versions of an assessment so that the publishers can gather norming data and assess the appropriateness of potential test items. To learn of field testing opportunities, teachers should visit the websites of publishers such as American Guidance Service or Harcourt Assessments, Inc.

MY TEACHER SAID Anecdotes for Classroom Reflection and Discussion

Sometimes the simplest assignments can lead to unexpected problems. The following anecdote describes a situation that occurred when a child was asked to bring her favorite book to school. Read and discuss this tale with your colleagues. What would you have done in this situation?

A Favorite Book

As they walked down the hall, first grade student Annie Scott proudly showed her mother a bulletin board with Annie's photograph, art work, and the short stories she had composed. Annie was the Student of the Week. This meant that her work was displayed for all her classmates to see and that Annie had the extra privilege of inviting a parent or special friend to school to read her favorite book to the class. Last week another student's father read *Where the Wild Things Are* to the class. Annie's friend Nina said that when it was her turn, she was going to ask her grandmother to read *Click, Clack, Moo, Cows That Type* because she thought that was a really funny book.

After greeting the teacher, Annie's mother took out a book and began to read from Psalm 23. "The Lord is my shepherd," she read, "I shall not want. He maketh me to lie down in green pastures: he leadeth me beside the still waters. He restoreth my soul: He leadeth me in the paths of righteousness for

His name's sake." "Excuse me," said the teacher, "I need to speak with you in the hall for a moment." When they were alone in the hallway, the teacher said, "We are not permitted to read Bible passages in a public school. Please read a different book to the children." "The Bible is Annie's favorite book," said Mrs. Scott, "You asked us to bring and read Annie's favorite book and we are completing your assignment. Annie has the right to hear her favorite book read in her own school." "Then I need permission from our principal," said the teacher, and he used the phone in his classroom to summon the principal.

The principal assessed the situation. "Adults are not permitted to read Bible passages aloud in the public schools. The children here respect you, Mrs. Scott, because you are Annie's mother. If you read to them from the Bible, you would have a great deal of influence upon them and that might conflict with the views of other parents and guardians. You can't read the Bible aloud in this school but I hope you will read a different book so that Annie can enjoy her time as Student of the Week."

Mrs. Scott was angry and wanted to walk out of the school. When she glanced at the bulletin board with Annie's work, however, she remembered Annie's excitement at being chosen Student of the Week. She didn't want to disappoint her daughter so she quickly grabbed a book from the classroom library and read to the class. Mrs. Scott planned to return and discuss the disagreement with the teacher and principal. Today, however, she would keep the argument away from the children and help her daughter celebrate her time as Student of the Week.

Questions

1. What could the teacher have done differently to prevent this conflict? Do you think he will rephrase the assignment during the next school year?
2. Did the teacher overreact by calling the principal or was he seeking appropriate guidance?
3. How can parents effectively participate in programs such as Student of the Week?

Lingering Thoughts: A Time for Reflection

1. What steps have I taken to improve my teaching? Have I attended weekend conferences, read professional literature, or enrolled in a course?
2. I encourage my students to read for recreation and to seek learning opportunities. Have I been modeling these practices?

References

Flournoy, V. (1985). *The patchwork quilt*. New York: Dial Books for Young Readers.

TEACHERS' RESOURCES

A Directory of Standards - 118

B Directory of Professional Organizations - - - - - - - - - - - 124

C Directory of Professional Journals and Periodicals - - - 131

D Directory of Free Materials for Teachers - - - - - - - - - - 143

E Directory of Resources for Inclusive Classrooms - - - - 149

F Directory of Websites for Elementary Teachers - - - - - - 153

A. Directory of Standards

The following professional organizations and websites can help teachers locate appropriate standards for professional development, lesson planning, and monitoring student progress. This standards directory has three sections:

I. Standards Expected for Student Teachers and Novice Teachers The standards listed in this section help beginning teachers know what administrators, parents, students, and peers expect of them in the classroom.

II. Standards Lists for Multiple Subject Areas This section lists organizations that provide standards for many subject areas and grade levels.

III. Standards Lists for Single Subject Areas In this section there are standards for single subject areas such as mathematics, reading/language arts, and social studies. Here teachers can find standards prepared by subject area organizations such as the National Council of Teachers of Mathematics (NCTM) and the International Reading Association (IRA).

I. STANDARDS EXPECTED FOR STUDENT TEACHERS AND NOVICE TEACHERS

1. Interstate New Teacher Assessment and Support Consortium Standards (INTASC)

The Interstate New Teacher Assessment and Support Consortium is a group of state education agencies and national educational organizations formed to prepare, license, and support the ongoing professional development of teachers. This consortium has published *Model Standards for Beginning Teacher Licensing, Assessment and Development: A Resource for State Dialogue.* The document outlines the essential knowledge, dispositions, and performance required for teachers at every grade level. Students in teacher preparation programs and novice teachers can find these standards by visiting the INTASC website.

Website: http://www.ccsso.org/projects/Interstate_New_Teacher_Assessment_and_Support_Consortium/Projects/Standards_Development/

2. National Board for Professional Teaching Standards

Many teachers seek National Board Certification. The National Board for Professional Teaching Standards (NBPTS) is an independent, nonprofit, nonpartisan organization led by a board of directors. The board of directors includes

You will find an electronic version of this material on the CD.

classroom teachers, school administrators, school board leaders, higher education officials, teacher union leaders, governors, and state legislators, as well as business and community leaders.
Website: http://www.nbpts.org/standards/stds.cfm
Telephone: 1-800-22TEACH (1-800-228-3224)

3. National Council for Accreditation of Teacher Education (NCATE)

The National Council for Accreditation of Teacher Education (NCATE) is a professional accreditation agency whose mission is to ensure that every student will have a qualified, knowledgeable teacher. To accomplish its mission, NCATE accredits teacher preparation institutions across the country and takes a leadership role in assuring that teachers can enhance and continue their education in Professional Development Schools and institutions of higher learning.
Website: http://www.ncate.org/standard/m_stds.ht

II. STANDARDS LISTS FOR MULTIPLE SUBJECT AREAS

1. Didax Educational Resources

Didax Educational Resources provides a comprehensive collection of standards in most curriculum areas. Topics addressed on the Didax website include: Mathematics, English/Language Arts, Arts, Technology, Science, Social Studies, Health, National Standards for Civics and Government, National Educational Goals, and State Standards.
Website: http://www.didax.com/standards/

2. Developing Educational Standards

The Developing Educational Standards website provides links to standards for every state. There are also links to standards by subject area.
Website: http://edstandards.org/Standards.html

3. Education World

The Education World website gives teachers quick and easy access to all state standards by grade level and topic. Teachers can click on the name of a state and find the standards for most curriculum areas.
Website: http://www.educationworld.com/standards/state/toc/index.shtml

4. McREL Standards

Standards addressing a multitude of subject areas and grade levels are available at the website of the Mid-continent Research for Education and Learning organization, McREL. McREL is a nationally recognized, nonprofit private organization that seeks to improve education through applied research, product development, and service.

Website: http://www.mcrel.org/

Mailing Address:
> Mid-continent Research for Education and Learning
> 2550 South Parker Road, Suite 500
> Aurora, CO 80014

Telephone: 303-337-0990

Fax: 303-337-3005

E-mail: info@mcrel.org

III. STANDARDS LISTS FOR SINGLE SUBJECT AREAS

1. Arts

National Standards for Art Education. The National Standards for Art Education lists standards in four arts areas: dance, music, theater, and the visual arts. Students should be able to meet these standards by completion of their secondary school experience. The standards for art education can be found by visiting the website for Didax Educational Resources listed below.

Website: http://www.didax.com/standards/arts/

2. Civics and Government

Center for Civic Education. National Standards for Civics and Government have been developed by the Center for Civic Education and funded by the U.S. Department of Education and the Pew Charitable Trusts. These standards guide teachers as they help their students develop the skills necessary to participate in a democratic society.

Website: http://www.civiced.org/stds.html

3. English Language Learners

Teachers of English to Speakers of Other Languages (TESOL). The Teachers of English to Speakers of Other Languages (TESOL) professional association has developed standards to guide the instruction of students from prekindergarten to twelfth grade who are learning English as a second or additional language. Teachers who are striving to give English language learners the most effective, appropriate instruction can visit their website to find standards and instructional techniques.

Website: http://www.tesol.edu/assoc/k12standards/it/01.html

4. Foreign Language Education

National Standards for Foreign Language Education. The American Council on the Teaching of Foreign Language (ACTFL) and several related agencies have developed national content standards for language education. Their goal is to help all students develop proficiency in English and at least one additional language, classical or modern, and to provide nonnative speakers of English with opportunities to become more proficient in their first language.
Website: http://www.actfl.org/public/articles/details.cfm?id=33

5. Health Education

American Association for Health Education. National health education standards have been developed by the American Association for Health Education. These standards explain the knowledge and behaviors students should exhibit in a healthy lifestyle. Teachers can find these standards by visiting the website given.
Website: http://www.aahperd.org/aahe/template.cfm?template=natl_health_education_standards.html

6. Mathematics

The National Council of Teachers of Mathematics. The National Council of Teachers of Mathematics (NCTM), founded in 1920, is the largest organization in the world dedicated to excellence in mathematics instruction. NCTM has published K-12 standards to guide teachers in planning effective mathematics instruction and assessing student progress. These standards are available at the website for the National Council of Teachers of Mathematics.
Website: http://www.standards.nctm.org

7. Music

National Standards for Music Education. By visiting the website for the National Association for Music Education, teachers can find the nine content standards for music education as well as additional resources for implementing the standards.
Website: http://www.menc.org/publication/books/standards.htm

8. Physical Education

National Association for Sport and Physical Education (NASPE). The National Association for Sport and Physical Education (NASPE) has published standards in their document *Moving into the Future: National Standards for*

Physical Education. This resource helps educators develop, implement, and evaluate kindergarten to twelfth grade physical education programs. The six content standards explained in this publication help teachers understand what students should know and demonstrate as a result of their participation in quality physical education programs.

Website: http://www.aahperd.org/naspe/template.cfm?template=pr_032504.html

9. Reading/Language Arts

International Reading Association/National Council of Teachers of English Standards (NCTE/IRA Standards). The International Reading Association (IRA) and the National Council of Teachers of English (NCTE) have copublished *Standards for the English Language Arts.*

An adapted list of the NCTE/IRA standards is available online. The complete volume, *Standards for the English Language Arts*, can be purchased through the International Reading Association.

Website: http://www.reading.org/advocacy/elastandards/standards.html

Order complete volume online: http://www.bookstore.reading.org

Mailing Address:
International Reading Association Order Department
800 Barksdale Road
PO Box 8139
Newark, DE 19714-8139

Telephone: 1-800-336-READ, ext. 266

Fax: 302-737-0878

10. Science

National Science Education Standards. The National Science Education Standards express goals for achievement that are appropriate for all members of the science community. Teachers can visit the website listed to find the standards as well as additional educational resources developed by the National Science Teachers Association.

Website: http://www.nsta.org/standards

11. Social Studies

National Council for the Social Studies. The National Council for the Social Studies (NCSS) has developed curriculum standards for kindergarten to twelfth grade. A complete copy of the NCSS Standards, *Expectations of Excellence: Curriculum Standards for Social Studies*, can be purchased by contacting:

Website: http://www.ncss.org/
Mailing Address:
>NCSS Publications
>P.O. Box 2067
>Waldorf, Maryland 20604-2067

Telephone: 1-800-683-0812

12. Technology

International Society for Technology in Education. The International Society for Technology in Education (ISTE) has developed standards for the most effective use of information technology in schools. Educators can find these standards by visiting the website listed.

Website: http://www.iste.org/standards/index.cfm

Mailing Address:
>ISTE—Customer Service
>480 Charnelton Street
>Eugene, OR 97401-2626

Phone: 800.336.5191 (U.S. and Canada)

Phone: 541.302.3777 (International)

Fax: 541.302.3778

E-mail: iste@iste.org

B. Directory of Professional Organizations

Professional organizations such as the International Reading Association (IRA), the National Council of Teachers of English (NCTE), the National Council of Teachers of Mathematics (NCTM), and the Association for Supervision and Curriculum Development (ASCD) can help teachers learn of developments in their field. Membership in these organizations offers teachers an opportunity to meet with colleagues and engage in research and service activities.

The Directory of Professional Organizations is divided into two sections:

I. **General Education Organizations** The first section describes and gives contact information for general educational organizations such as Kappa Delta Pi whose membership includes teachers of all subject areas and grade levels.

II. **Educational Organizations Serving a Specific Group of Teachers** The second section gives contact information and descriptions of organizations that serve a specific group of teachers. Here teachers will find organizations such as the Council for Exceptional Children (CEC), which works with teachers engaged in special education, as well as the National Association for the Education of Young Children (NAEYC), which serves teachers of children from birth to the primary grades.

I. GENERAL EDUCATION ORGANIZATIONS

1. The Association for Supervision and Curriculum Development (ASCD)

The Association for Supervision and Curriculum Development is an internationally recognized nonprofit organization serving school administrators, teachers, and students at all grade levels.

Website: http://www.ascd.org

Mailing Address:

Association for Supervision and Curriculum Development
1703 North Beauregard Street
Alexandria, VA 22311-1714

Telephone: 703-578-9600

Fax: 703-575-5400

E-mail: member@ascd.org

You will find an electronic version of this material on the CD.

2. Kappa Delta Pi

Kappa Delta Pi, the International Honor Society in Education, is an organization composed of new and veteran teachers who join together to complete service projects in education, celebrate the profession with intriguing research and publications, and support members in career advancement.

Many educators join Kappa Delta Pi through a chapter based at a university. Individuals who are unable to join an institutional chapter, alumni chapter, or school chapter may apply to become members at large.

Website: http://www.kdp.org

Mailing Address:
> Kappa Delta Pi
> 3707 Woodview Trace
> Indianapolis, IN 46268-1158

Telephone: 800-284-3167

3. Phi Delta Kappa

Professional educators can join Phi Delta Kappa, an international association that promotes quality education by offering professional development, networking opportunities, and innovative research to its members.

Website: http://www.pdkintl.org/

Mailing Address:
> Phi Delta Kappa International
> 408 North Union Street
> P.O. Box 789
> Bloomington, Indiana 47402-0789

Telephone: Monday–Friday 8:00 A.M.–5:00 P.M. EST (Summer hours 8:00 A.M. – 4:30 P.M.) 800/766-1156; 812/339-1156

Fax: 812/339-0018

E-mail: information@pdkintl.org

II. EDUCATIONAL ORGANIZATIONS SERVING A SPECIFIC GROUP OF TEACHERS

1. Teachers Working with English Language Learners

Teachers of English to Speakers of Other Languages (TESOL). Teachers of English to Speakers of Other Languages (TESOL), a professional organization, strives to bring high-quality English language education to individuals who are learning English as a second or additional language. TESOL encourages respect for diversity and multiculturalism, collaborative projects, and reflective instructional practices. TESOL has approximately 14,000 members residing in over 120 countries.

Website: http://www.tesol.org

Mailing Address:
> Teachers of English to Speakers of Other Languages
> 700 South Washington Street, Suite 200
> Alexandria, VA 22314

Telephone: 888-547-3369 or 703-836-0774

Fax: 703-836-7864 or 703-836-6447

2. Teachers Working With Students With Special Needs

Council for Exceptional Children. The Council for Exceptional Children (CEC) is a professional organization that works to improve educational opportunities for individuals with exceptionalities, students with disabilities, and/or the gifted. CEC offers its members access to professional development, print and online resources, and opportunities to meet and discuss concerns with novice and veteran educators.

Website: http://www.cec.sped.org

Mailing Address:
> The Council for Exceptional Children (CEC)
> 1110 North Glebe Road, Suite 300
> Arlington, VA 22201

Telephone (voice): 703-620-3660

Telephone (TTY): 866-915-5000

Fax: 703-264-9494

E-mail: service@cec.sped.org

3. Teachers of Young Children

National Association for the Education of Young Children (NAEYC). Teachers working with young children (infants to the primary grades) will find informative journals as well as quality professional development programs and resources when they join the National Association for the Education of Young Children (NAEYC). Since 1926, NAEYC has been striving to build public awareness and support for high-quality early childhood programs. The group strives to bring better services for young children and to improve working conditions and professional support for their teachers.

Website: http://www.naeyc.org

Mailing Address:
> National Association for the Education of Young Children
> 1509 16th Street NW
> Washington, DC 20036

Telephone: 800-424-2460
E-mail: membership@naeyc.org

4. Teachers of Middle School Students

National Middle School Students Association. Since 1973, the National Middle School Students Association has been supporting educators who work with young adolescents. The association offers conferences and publications that help middle school teachers meet the needs of their students.
Website: http://www.nmsa.org
Mailing Address:
  National Middle School Association
  4151 Executive Parkway, Suite 300
  Westerville, OH 43081
Telephone: 1-800-528-NMSA (6672) or 614-895-4730
Fax: 614-895-4750
E-mail: info@NMSA.org

5. Art Teachers

National Art Education Association. The National Art Education Association, founded in 1947, supports art education by offering professional development opportunities, scholarly journals, and additional resources for a diverse group of educators.
Website: http://www.naea-reston.org
Mailing Address:
  National Art Education Association
  1916 Association Drive
  Reston, VA 20191-1590
Telephone: 703-860-8000
Fax: 703-860-2960

6. Health and Physical Education Teachers

American Association for Health, Physical Education, Recreation & Dance. The American Association for Health, Physical Education, Recreation & Dance encourages the professional development of teachers in the fields of physical education, leisure, fitness, dance, and other specialties related to achieving a healthy lifestyle. Membership in this association enables teachers to receive professional journals and participate in conferences.
Website: http://www.aahperd.org/aahperd/template.cfm?template=aahperd_about.html

Mailing Address:
American Alliance for Health, Physical Education, Recreation & Dance
1900 Association Drive
Reston, VA 20191-1598

Telephone: 703-476-3400

7. Mathematics Teachers

The National Council of Teachers of Mathematics (NCTM). The National Council of Teachers of Mathematics (NCTM) is the largest nonprofit professional association dedicated to providing quality mathematics instruction to students in kindergarten to twelfth grade as well as in higher education. NCTM members have opportunities to attend national and regional conferences, read and write for professional journals, and attend workshops for continual professional development.

Website: http://www.nctm.org

Mailing Address:
National Council of Teachers of Mathematics
1906 Association Drive
Drawer A
Reston, VA 20191-1502

Telephone: 800-235-7566
Fax: 703-476-2970

8. Music Teachers

Music Teachers National Association. The Music Teachers National Association (MTNA) offers resources for music teachers at every grade level. The association strives to enhance the quality of music education throughout the country.

Website: http://www.mtna.org

Mailing Address:
Music Teachers National Association
441 Vine Street, Suite 505
Cincinnati, OH 45202

Telephone: 513-421-1420 or 888-512-5278
Fax: 513-421-2503

9. Reading and Language Arts Teachers

The International Reading Association. The International Reading Association offers many print and electronic journals, regional and international conferences, and powerful position statements to guide literacy teachers at all levels.

Website: http://www.reading.org

Mailing Address:
International Reading Association
800 Barksdale Road
P.O. Box 6021
Newark, DE 19714-6021

Telephone: 800-628-8508, ext. 290

Fax: 302-737-0878

The National Council of Teachers of English. The National Council of Teachers of English has been meeting the needs of literacy teachers since 1911. This organization serves teachers at all scholastic levels with journals, conferences, and Internet resources.

Website: http://www.ncte.org

Mailing Address:
National Council of Teachers of English
Customer Service
1111 West Kenyon Road
Urbana, IL 61801

Telephone: 877-369-6283

Fax: 217-328-9645

10. Science Teachers

The National Science Teachers Association. The National Science Teachers Association (NSTA) encourages excellence and innovation in science classrooms. The association publishes a professional journal for each scholastic level (elementary, middle, and high school) and holds conferences for educators to meet and share instructional techniques and research.

Website: http://www.nsta.org

Mailing Address:
National Science Teachers Association
1840 Wilson Boulevard
Arlington, VA 22201-3000

Telephone: 703-243-7100

11. Social Studies Teachers

National Council for the Social Studies. Founded in 1921, the National Council for the Social Studies supports and provides leadership and service to social studies educators working with students from kindergarten to higher education.

Website: http://www.socialstudies.org

Mailing Address:
    National Council for the Social Studies
    8555 16th Street
    Silver Spring, Maryland 20910

Telephone: 800-296-7840

Fax: 301-588-2049

C. Directory of Professional Journals and Periodicals

Novice and veteran teachers can learn of new research, trends, and instructional methodology by reading professional journals. This directory of professional literature can help teachers maintain a current perspective on educational issues.

The Professional Journals and Periodicals Directory is divided into seven sections to help teachers find the most appropriate resources:

I. Journals and Periodicals for a General Education Audience

II. Journals and Periodicals for Early Childhood Educators

III. Journals and Periodicals for Elementary Teachers

IV. Journals and Periodicals for Middle School Teachers

V. Journals and Periodicals for Teachers of Students with Special Needs

VI. Journals and Periodicals for Teachers of English Language Learners (ELL)

VII. Subject-Specific Journals and Periodicals

I. JOURNALS AND PERIODICALS FOR A GENERAL EDUCATION AUDIENCE

1. *Classroom Leadership*

Classroom Leadership is a newsletter published nine times per year by the Association for Supervision and Curriculum Development (ASCD). *Classroom Leadership* is written by teachers for teachers and contains advice and strategies teachers can use immediately in their classrooms.

Website: http://www.ascd.org

Mailing Address:
Association for Supervision and Curriculum Development
1703 North Beauregard Street
Alexandria, VA 22311

Telephone: 800-933-ASCD or 703-578-9600

You will find an electronic version of this material on the CD.

2. *Education Week*

The weekly newspaper for K–12 educators, *Education Week*, offers information on trends, employment opportunities, and innovative programs for teachers and administrators.

Website: http://www.educationweek.org

Mailing Address:
    Education Week
    6935 Arlington Road, Suite 100
    Bethesda, MD 20814-5233

Telephone: 800-728-2790

Fax: 740-389-6720

3. *The New Teacher Advocate*

The New Teacher Advocate is published quarterly by Kappa Delta Pi, the International Honor Society in Education. This newsletter supports new teachers with practical advice and first-person stories from teachers at every grade level.

Website: http://www.kdp.org

Mailing Address:
    Kappa Delta Pi
    3707 Woodview Trace
    Indianapolis, IN 46268-1158

Telephone: 800-284-3167

4. *Teacher Magazine*

Teacher Magazine deals with controversial issues in K–12 education such as tracking, job security for teachers, and the ramifications of the No Child Left Behind legislation. There are also listings of grant opportunities, conferences, and professional vacancies. These features plus the book reviews, first-person accounts, and technology articles make *Teacher Magazine* thought-provoking reading for all educators.

Website: http://www.teachermagazine.org/

Mailing Address:
    Teacher Magazine
    6935 Arlington Road
    Bethesda, MD 20814

Telephone: 800-728-2753

Fax: 740-389-6720

E-mail: tm@epe.org

5. *Technology & Learning Magazine*

Technology & Learning Magazine contains articles that describe innovative instructional approaches and unique ways to use technology in classrooms at every grade level.

Website: http://www.techlearning.com

Mailing Address:
> Technology & Learning
> Subscription Department
> P.O. Box 5052
> Vandalia, OH 45377

Telephone: 800-607-4410

6. *T. H. E. Journal: Technological Horizons in Education*

T.H.E. Journal demystifies technology for teachers and administrators and helps educators at every grade level make purchasing and instructional decisions. Free subscription to this journal is available to educators in the United States.

Website: http://www.thejournal.com

Mailing Address:
> T.H.E. Journal
> 1750 17th Street, Suite 230
> Tustin, CA 92780

II. JOURNALS AND PERIODICALS FOR EARLY CHILDHOOD EDUCATORS

1. *Young Children*

Young Children is a peer-reviewed journal published by the National Association for the Education of Young Children (NAEYC). This journal offers research, theory, and instructional practices of interest to teachers of children from birth to the primary grades.

Website: http://www.naeyc.org

Mailing Address:
> National Association for the Education of Young Children
> 1509 16th Street NW
> Washington, D.C. 20036

Telephone: 800-424-2460 or 202-232-8777

Fax: 202-328-1846

2. *Early Childhood Research Quarterly*

A scholarly journal of the National Association for the Education of Young Children, *Early Childhood Research Quarterly*, offers research and "Practitioner Perspectives" that comment on that research.

Website: http://www.naeyc.org

Mailing Address:
> National Association for the Education of Young Children
> 1509 16th Street NW
> Washington, D.C. 20036

Telephone: 800-424-2460 or 202-232-8777

Fax: 202-328-1846

III. JOURNALS AND PERIODICALS FOR ELEMENTARY TEACHERS

1. *Creative Classroom*

Creative Classroom magazine is published by the Children's Television Workshop. The magazine features resources for teachers of grades K–8 and contains reproducible pages, projects, and educational news.

Website: http://www.creativeclassroom.org/

Mailing Address:
> Creative Classroom
> 149 5th Avenue, 12th Floor
> New York, NY 10010

Telephone: 1-800-759-6383

2. *Instructor*

Instructor offers a wealth of standards-based lesson plans, classroom activities, and suggestions for involving parents in their children's elementary education.

Website: http://www.scholastic.com/instructor

Mailing Address:
> Instructor
> 555 Broadway
> New York, NY 10012-3999

Telephone: 1-800-544-2917

3. *The Mailbox*

The Mailbox magazine contains lesson plans, unit plans, and a variety of activities. There are grade-specific editions enabling teachers to choose from the Preschool, Kindergarten, Primary (grades 1–3) or Intermediate (grades 4–6) editions.

Website: http://www.themailbox.com

Mailing Address:
The Mailbox Magazine
P.O. Box 51676
Boulder, CO 80323-1676

Telephone: 1-800-627-8579

4. *Teaching PreK–8*

Teaching PreK-8 contains information on children's literature, classroom activities, and articles profiling innovative schools and instructional practices.

Website: http://www.TeachingK-8.com

Mailing Address:
Teaching PreK-8
P.O. Box 54805
Boulder, CO 80323-4805

Telephone: 1-800-678-8793

IV. JOURNALS AND PERIODICALS FOR MIDDLE SCHOOL TEACHERS

1. *Middle School Journal*

Middle School Journal, published five times per year, is a journal that addresses the needs of educators working with 10- to 15-year-old students. There are thematic and general topic issues to help teachers learn of theory and practice in middle school education.

Website: http://www.nmsa.org

Mailing Address:
Middle School Journal
National Middle School Association
4151 Executive Parkway, Suite 300
Westerville, OH 43081

Telephone: 1-800-528-NMSA or 614-895-4730
Fax: 614-895-4750

2. *Middle Ground*

Middle Ground is published four times per year by the National Middle School Association. This is a practitioner-oriented periodical that offers instructional suggestions and advice for the middle school educator.

Website: http://www.nmsa.org

Mailing Address:
>Middle School Journal
>National Middle School Association
>4151 Executive Parkway, Suite 300
>Westerville, OH 43081

Telephone: 1-800-528-NMSA or 614-895-4730

Fax: 614-895-4750

V. JOURNALS AND PERIODICALS FOR TEACHERS OF STUDENTS WITH SPECIAL NEEDS

1. *Exceptional Children*

Published four times per year by the Council for Exceptional Children, *Exceptional Children* is a peer-reviewed journal of original research on the development of infants, toddlers, children, and youth with special needs.

Website: http://www.cec.sped.org

Mailing Address:
>Council for Exceptional Children
>1110 North Glebe Road
>Arlington, VA 22201-5704

Telephone (voice): 1-888-CEC-SPED or 703-620-3660

Telephone (TTY): 703-264-9446

2. *Learning Disabilities Quarterly*

A publication of the Council for Learning Disabilities, the *Learning Disabilities Quarterly*, offers research that can help teachers of students with special needs use the most effective instructional methods.

Website: http://www.cldinternational.org

Mailing Address:
>Council for Learning Disabilities
>P.O. Box 4014
>Leesburg, VA 20177

Telephone: 571-258-1010

Fax: 571-258-1011

VI. JOURNALS AND PERIODICALS FOR TEACHERS OF ENGLISH LANGUAGE LEARNERS (ELL)

The following journals are published by TESOL, Teachers of English to Speakers of Other Languages, and can be helpful to teachers working with English Language Learners (ELL).

Website: http://www.tesol.org

Mailing Address:
700 South Washington Street, Suite 200
Alexandria, VA 22314

Telephone: 888-547-3369 or 703-836-0774

Fax: 703-836-7864 or 703-836-6447

1. *TESOL Quarterly*

TESOL Quarterly is a scholarly journal for educators working with individuals who are learning English as an additional language.

2. *Essential Teacher*

Essential Teacher is a practical magazine dedicated to helping teachers apply the most effective instructional techniques when working with English Language Learners.

3. *TESOL Connections*

TESOL Connections is a newsletter of headlines and resource links to materials related to second language acquisition.

VII. SUBJECT-SPECIFIC JOURNALS AND PERIODICALS

1. Reading and Language Arts Teachers

The Reading Teacher. Published by the International Reading Association, *The Reading Teacher* is a peer-reviewed journal that serves individuals interested in children's literacy learning. *The Reading Teacher* offers discussions of instructional procedures, articles related to literacy instruction, and reviews of professional literature and children's literature. *The Reading Teacher* addresses topics of interest to teachers of kindergarten to grade 6.

Website: http://www.reading.org

Mailing Address:
The Reading Teacher
800 Barksdale Road

P.O. Box 8139
Newark, DE 19714-8139
Telephone: 1-800-731-1600, ext. 267

The Journal of Adolescent and Adult Literacy. *The Journal of Adolescent and Adult Literacy* is a peer-reviewed journal published by the International Reading Association. The journal contains theory, research, and instructional practices related to the literacy development of adolescents and adults.

Website: http://www.reading.org

Mailing Address:
The Journal of Adolescent and Adult Literacy
800 Barksdale Road
P.O. Box 8139
Newark, DE 19714-8139

Telephone: 1-800-731-1600, ext. 267

Reading Research Quarterly. *Reading Research Quarterly*, a peer-reviewed journal, is published by the International Reading Association. It offers studies related to literacy development.

Website: http://www.reading.org

Mailing Address:
Reading Research Quarterly
800 Barksdale Road
P.O. Box 8139
Newark, DE 19714-8139

Telephone: 1-800-731-1600, ext. 267

Language Arts. A professional journal for elementary and middle school teachers, *Language Arts*, offers articles on theory and classroom practices, current research, and reviews of instructional materials and literature.

Website: http://www.ncte.org

Mailing Address:
National Council of Teachers of English
1111 West Kenyon Road
Urbana, IL 61801-1096

Telephone: 217-328-3870 or 877-369-6283

Voices From the Middle. Each issue of *Voices from the Middle* is devoted to one literacy topic for middle school education. There are descriptions of authentic classroom practices, reviews of adolescent literature, and technology updates.

Website: http://www.ncte.org

Mailing Address:
>National Council of Teachers of English
>1111 West Kenyon Road
>Urbana, IL 61801-1096

Telephone: 217-328-3870 or 877-369-6283

English Journal. Senior high school and middle school teachers can find reviews of classroom materials as well as research and theory in *English Journal*, a bimonthly publication of the National Council of Teachers of English.

Website: http://www.ncte.org

Mailing Address:
>National Council of Teachers of English
>1111 West Kenyon Road
>Urbana, IL 61801-1096

Telephone: 217-328-3870 or 877-369-6283

2. Art Teachers

Art Education: The Journal of the National Art Education Association. Art *Education* is published bimonthly by the National Art Education Association. This journal addresses the needs of a diverse audience. Each issue addresses a specific theme or topic and contains practical information for teachers at all grade levels.

Website: http://www.naea-reston.org

Mailing Address:
>National Art Education Association
>1916 Association Drive
>Reston, VA 20191-1590

Telephone: 703-860-8000

Fax: 703-860-2960

3. Health and Physical Education Teachers

The American Association for Health, Physical Education, Recreation & Dance publishes journals to further the professional development of its members. Teachers can subscribe to these journals by contacting The American Association for Health, Physical Education, Recreation & Dance.

Website: http://www.aahperd.org/aahperd/template.cfm?template=aahperd_about.html

Mailing Address:
>American Alliance for Health, Physical Education, Recreation & Dance
>1900 Association Drive
>Reston, VA 20191-1598

Telephone: 703-476-3400

Journal of Physical Education, Recreation, & Dance. The *Journal of Physical Education, Recreation, & Dance* is published monthly and addresses the needs of teachers in all areas related to maintaining a healthy lifestyle.

Strategies: A Journal for Physical & Sports Educators. *Strategies: A Journal for Physical & Sports Educators* is a peer-reviewed journal published six times per year. The articles and features address the needs of educators dealing with all levels of physical education.

4. Music Teachers

American Music Teacher Magazine. *American Music Teacher Magazine* provides articles and instructional ideas for music teachers at every grade level.

Website: http://www.mtna.org

Mailing Address:
Music Teachers National Association
441 Vine Street, Suite 505
Cincinnati, OH 45202

Telephone: 513-421-1420 or 888-512-5278

Fax: 513-421-2503

5. Mathematics Teachers

The following journals are published by the National Council of Teachers of Mathematics (NCTM). These publications present research and help teachers implement effective instructional techniques in mathematics education. Teachers can subscribe to these journals by contacting the National Council of Teachers of Mathematics.

Website: http://www.nctm.org

Mailing Address:
National Council of Teachers of Mathematics
1906 Association Drive
Drawer A
Reston, VA 20191-1502

Telephone: 800-235-7566

Fax: 703-476-2970

Teaching Children Mathematics (TCM). *Teaching Children Mathematics* (TCM) is a monthly journal designed for teachers in elementary schools.

Mathematics Teaching in the Middle School (MTMS). *Mathematics Teaching in the Middle School* (MTMS) is a monthly journal that addresses the concerns of middle school teachers.

Mathematics Teacher (MT). *Mathematics Teacher* (MT) is a monthly journal devoted to topics that would interest high school teachers.

Online Journal for School Mathematics (ON-Math). *Online Journal for School Mathematics* (ON-Math) is a peer-reviewed school journal that is only available online.

Journal for Research in Mathematics Education (JRME). *Journal for Research in Mathematics Education* (JRME) is a research journal for math educators in kindergarten to grade 12 as well as in higher education.

6. Science Teachers

The following journals are published by the National Science Teachers Association (NSTA). These journals help teachers provide effective, age-appropriate science instruction to students at all grade levels. Teachers can subscribe to these journals by contacting the National Science Teachers Association.

Website: http://www.nsta.org

Mailing Address:
National Science Teachers Association
1840 Wilson Boulevard
Arlington, VA 22201-3000

Telephone: 703-243-7100

Science and Children. *Science and Children* is the National Science Teachers Association's professional journal for teachers in the elementary schools.

Science Scope. *Science Scope* is a professional journal that addresses the needs of middle school science teachers.

The Science Teacher. *The Science Teacher* contains articles of interest to high school science teachers.

7. Social Studies

The National Council for the Social Studies publishes journals to encourage teachers' professional development. Educators can contact The National Council for the Social Studies to subscribe to the following publications.

Website: http://www.socialstudies.org

Mailing Address:
National Council for the Social Studies
8555 16th Street
Silver Spring, Maryland 20910

Telephone: 800-296-7840

Fax: 301-588-2049

Social Education. *Social Education* provides a balance of practical ideas and theory for social studies teachers at all levels. This journal is published seven times per year.

Social Studies and the Young Learner. Teachers of kindergarten to grade six can find helpful articles and classroom profiles in *Social Studies and the Young Learner. Social Studies and the Young Learner* is published quarterly.

Middle Level Learning. Published three times each year, *Middle Level Learning* helps middle school teachers find age-appropriate classroom practices and methodology to enhance social studies education.

D. Directory of Free Materials for Teachers

You're ready to enter the classroom with knowledge of standards, an understanding of child development, and a well-developed philosophy of education. Now you need the supplies to enable you to implement your plans.

You may be fortunate to work in a school with an abundance of materials. At times, however, you may seek items that are not easily found in your school's supply closet or the local teachers' resource store. This section suggests sources of free materials to enhance instruction and brighten the classroom environment. This directory is divided into three sections:

I. Local Sources of Free Materials for Teachers

II. Corporate-Sponsored Programs for Education

III. Government-Sponsored Programs for Education

I. LOCAL SOURCES OF FREE MATERIALS FOR TEACHERS

1. Book Store Displays

Do you search for pictures to brighten your library corner or bulletin board? Have your students become hooked on book series such as Harry Potter, Lemony Snickets, or Artemis Fowl? Bookstores usually receive promotional displays featuring large color photos of literary characters such as Junie B. Jones and Clifford, The Big Red Dog. Often the bookstores discard these materials when the promotions end. Savvy teachers contact bookstore managers and request decorations that are destined for disposal. Many bookstore managers are eager to distribute the free bookmarks, notecards, and posters they receive from publishers. Such an exchange identifies the bookstore as a good neighbor in the community and encourages families to visit the bookstore.

2. Movie Posters

The Polar Express, *Because of Winn-Dixie*, *Stuart Little*, *Holes*, and *Harry Potter*! The best titles in children's literature have come to the silver screen. Teachers seeking colorful posters for a classroom library corner can ask movie theaters and DVD/Video Rental Agencies to donate movie posters and promotional materials after they have been displayed. After seeing a film, students may be motivated to read the book and compare the film and text versions.

You will find an electronic version of this material on the CD.

3. Envelopes and Greeting Cards

A gift shop owner had a dilemma. When buying greeting cards, his customers often shopped hastily and picked up envelopes that didn't match the cards they were buying. At the end of each month, the storeowner had a large pile of mismatched cards and envelopes. The storeowner decided to give the envelopes to teachers in his community. With these free materials, children learned to address envelopes and exchange greetings with pen pals. Teachers might consider asking store owners in their communities to donate mismatched envelopes for similar projects.

4. Travel Agencies

Travel agencies often have brochures, posters, videotapes, and DVDs that can help teachers bring the wonders of the world to their classrooms. Travel materials can be used to create word problems in mathematics classrooms, spark short stories in language arts classrooms, or illustrate geographical terms in social studies classrooms. Teachers can visit travel agencies to request materials for classroom use.

II. CORPORATE-SPONSORED PROGRAMS FOR EDUCATION

1. Campbell's Labels for Education

Since 1973, the Campbell's Labels for Education program has been helping schools acquire sports equipment and educational merchandise such as computers, software, videocassettes, and library and reference materials. Students, parents, and other members of the community work together to gather labels, lids, and/or UPC codes from eligible products. Schools then exchange the labels for merchandise from the Campbell's catalog.

Website: http://www.labelsforeducation.com
Telephone: 1-800-424-5331 (The phone lines are open from 8:00 A.M. to 5:30 P.M. CST.)

2. Funding Factory

The Funding Factory helps nonprofit organizations acquire equipment and cash by recycling used cell phones and empty inkjet and laser cartridges. Schools can register with the program and learn details by visiting the website.

Website: http://www.fundingfactory.com

3. General Mills Box Tops for Education

Schools can acquire needed funds by collecting and redeeming box tops from eligible General Mills products. There are many ways to participate in this program and school coordinators should visit the website to consider all of the options.

Website: http://www.boxtops4education.com

Mailing Address:
Box Tops for Education
P.O. Box 8998
Young America, MN 55551

Telephone: 1-888-799-2444 (The phone lines are open from 7:00 A.M. to 7:00 P.M. CST, 7 days per week.)

Fax: 1-800-353-1341

4. The Newspaper Association of America Foundation/Newspaper in Education

The Newspaper in Education (NIE) is an international program helping teachers bring local, national, and international events to their classrooms since 1955. Through this program, businesses are encouraged to provide funds so that schools can receive newspapers on a regular basis. Teachers who wish to have newspapers delivered to their classroom can visit the NIE website to find participating newspapers in their area.

Website: http://www.naa.org/foundation/nie.html

Telephone: 703-902-1730

Fax Numbers: 703-902-1735/1736

5. Pizza Hut BOOK IT! National Reading Incentive Program

Since 1985, the Pizza Hut BOOK IT! National Reading Incentive Program has been awarding free personal pan pizzas to students in kindergarten to grade six when they reach their reading goals. The program is individualized and encourages teachers and students to work together to set personal reading goals. These goals can include accomplishments such as participating in literature circles, reading a particular number of pages or books in one month, or reading for an established length of time every day. When a student reaches his monthly reading goal, he receives a certificate that can be redeemed at a Pizza Hut restaurant for a free personal pan pizza. Students can earn one pizza each month from October to March. Approximately 895,000 classrooms participate in the annual BOOK IT! Program.

Website: www.bookitprogram.com

Telephone: 1-800-4-BOOKIT

6. Pizza Hut BOOK IT! Beginners Program

Since 1998, the Pizza Hut BOOK IT! Beginners Program has encouraged early childhood educators to read to their classes by offering supportive reading resource materials and free pizza certificates. Teachers in preschools, prekindergartens, or licensed child care facilities with a minimum of four students between the ages of three and five can enroll in the Pizza Hut BOOK IT! Beginners Program.

To participate, teachers enroll and agree to read to their classes for a minimum of 60 minutes each week during the months of March and April. After each four-week reading period, the children are given certificates they can exchange for a free personal pan pizza at a Pizza Hut restaurant.

Website: http://www.bookitbeginners.com/
Telephone: 1-800-4-BOOKIT

7. *T.H.E. Journal: Technological Horizons in Education*

Teachers in the United States can subscribe to T.H.E. Journal: Technological Horizons in Education with no cost. This monthly periodical offers teachers guidance in obtaining grants, purchasing equipment, and using technology wisely.

Website: http://www.thejournal.com
Mailing Address:
T.H.E. Journal
17501 17th Street, Suite 230
Tustin, CA 92780

8. The World of Mouse/Free Mouse Pads

Accredited K–12 schools, colleges, and universities can receive free advertiser-supported mouse pads for their computer stations from the Word of Mouse company. To receive the mouse pads, educators join a waiting list by registering their schools at the Word of Mouse website, http://gomouse.westside.com/SchoolSignup/default.view. Organizations wishing to sponsor schools examine the list and select schools based upon factors such as a school's location and demographics. More than 6,000 schools have received free materials from Word of Mouse.

Website: http://gomouse.westside.com/SchoolSignup/default.view
Telephone: 212-253-1811

III. GOVERNMENT-SPONSORED PROGRAMS FOR EDUCATION

1. Captioned Media Program

With funding from the U.S. Department of Education, the Captioned Media Program (CMP) distributes open-captioned media to individuals with hearing impairments as well as teachers and other professionals who work with this population. (When an open-captioned film is played on a standard VCR or DVD player, the captions appear automatically. No special equipment is needed to show the captions.) Teachers who register with the Captioned Media Program receive a catalog with titles and descriptions of over 4,000 captioned videotapes, CD-ROMS, and DVDs available on a free-loan basis. There are no registration, rental, or postage fees for individuals using this service. Materials can be ordered online or by telephone. Many of the captioned educational videos also come with printed lesson plans.

Website: http://www.cfv.org

Mailing Address:
Captioned Media Program
National Association of the Deaf
1447 East Main Street
Spartanburg, SC 29307

Telephone (voice): 800-237-6213

Telephone (TTY): 800-237-6819

Fax: 800-538-5636

E-mail: info@cfv.org

2. The National Institute for Literacy

The National Institute for Literacy makes a variety of reports available on its website, http://www.nifl.gov. Teachers can also order hard copies of the reports by calling the National Institute for Literacy at EDPubs at 1-800-228-8813 (TDD/TTY1-877-576-7734) or by using the fax number 1-301-470-1244.

3. The Partnership for Reading

The Partnership for Reading is a collaborative effort of the National Institute for Literacy, the National Institute of Child Health and Human Development, the U.S. Department of Health and Human Services, and the U.S. Department of Education. To improve reading instruction for children and adults, the Partnership for Reading makes scientifically based research available to the public.

Website: http://www.nifl.gov/partnershipforreading

Mailing Address:
Partnership for Reading
1775 I Street NW, Suite 730
Washington, D.C. 2006

4. National Library Service for the Blind and Physically Handicapped (NLS)

The National Library Service for the Blind and Physically Handicapped offers free loan of recorded magazines and books, the equipment to play the recordings, described videos, large print books, and Braille materials to individuals with a visual impairment, physical disability, or physically based reading disability that hinders their ability to read standard print materials. Upon acceptance into the program, requested materials are sent to the patron's home in a package that includes return postage. Individuals using this program incur no costs for rentals or postage.

Website: http://www.loc.gov/nls/

Telephone: 202-707-5100

Toll-Free Telephone: 1-888-NLS-READ or 1-888-657-7323 (to connect to a local library)

TDD: 202-707-0744

Fax: 202-707-0712

# E. Directory of Resources for Inclusive Classrooms

Teachers in inclusive classrooms strive to make every child feel respected and successful. The private organizations and government programs listed in this directory offer instructional materials, parent guides, and research to help teachers provide the most appropriate instruction for students with special needs.

This directory is divided into two sections:

I. Resources for Students with Visual Impairments or Print Disabilities

II. Resources for Students with Hearing Impairments

I. RESOURCES FOR STUDENTS WITH VISUAL IMPAIRMENTS OR PRINT DISABILITIES

1. Recording for the Blind & Dyslexic (RFB&D)

The private, nonprofit organization, Recording for the Blind & Dyslexic (RFB&D), offers audio versions of textbooks as well as related library services to individuals with print disabilities.

Website: http://www.rfbd.org

Mailing Address:
Recording for the Blind & Dyslexic
20 Roszel Road
Princeton, NJ 08540

Telephone: 1-800-221-4792

2. National Library Service for the Blind and Physically Handicapped

The National Library Service for the Blind and Physically Handicapped provides books as well as subscriptions to magazines such as *Cricket*, *National Geographic World*, *Spider*, *Sports Illustrated for Kids*, and *Teen People* free to students with visual or print disabilities. The material is delivered in an audio format.

Website: http://www.loc.gov/nls/

Mailing Address:
National Library Service for the Blind and Physically Handicapped
Library of Congress
Washington, DC 20542

You will find an electronic version of this material on the CD.

Telephone: 202-707-5100
Toll-Free Telephone: 1-800-424-8567
TDD: 202-707-0744
Fax: 202-707-0712
E-mail: nlswebmaster@loc.gov

3. Library Reproduction Service

Large print textbooks can be purchased from the Library Reproduction Service.
Website: http://www.lrs-largeprint.com/home.html
Mailing Address:
Library Reproduction Service
14214 South Figueroa Street
Los Angeles, CA 90061
Telephone: 1-800-255-5002
E-mail: lrsprint@aol.com

4. American Printing House for the Blind

The American Printing House for the Blind offers large print as well as Braille editions of textbooks.
Mailing Address:
American Printing House for the Blind
1839 Frankfort Avenue
P.O. Box 6085
Louisville, KY 40206-0085
Telephone: 502-895-2405
Toll-Free Customer Service: 1-800-223-1839
Fax: 502-899-2274
E-mail: info@aph.org

5. National Braille Association (NBA)

Braille textbook editions can be obtained by contacting the National Braille Association (NBA).
Website: http://www.nationalbraille.org
Mailing Address:
National Braille Association
Braille Materials Production Center
Three Townline Circle
Rochester, NY 14623-2513
Telephone: 585-427-8260
E-mail: nbaoffice@nationalbraille.org

6. National Organization of Parents of Blind Children: Slate Pals/Pen Pals for Students Who Use Braille

Sponsored by the National Organization of Parents of Blind Children, Slate Pals helps students with visual impairments find pen pals. This is a program in which Braille-reading students can write and receive letters from other students who are learning to use Braille. Students who enroll in the program can specify whether they would like to correspond with a boy or a girl and the age range of the pen pal they would like to have. Teachers who would like to enroll students in this program can contact the National Organization of Parents of Blind Children.

Mailing Address:
Slate Pals
5817 North Niam
Chicago, IL 60631

E-mail: dkent@ripco.com

7. Descriptive Video Service

When a class is watching a film, a student with a visual impairment may listen to the film and glean what he can from the dialog. That student, however, may hear sounds such as running footsteps and wonder which of the film's characters is running. Described programming provides narration that students with visual impairments can use to help them understand a film. When a film is described, visual elements such as scenery or a character's costume or gestures are described on a second audio track.

Like captioned programming, described programming was developed to help individuals with disabilities. Educators are finding, however, that described programming can enhance comprehension for all students.

Teachers who wish to learn more about described programming can contact Descriptive Video Service at WGBH, the Public Broadcasting Service (PBS) station in Boston, Massachusetts.

Website: http://www.dvs.wgbh.org

Mailing Address:
Descriptive Video Service
WGBH
125 Western Avenue
Boston, MA 02134

Telephone: 617-300-3600

E-mail: dvs@wgbh.org

Described films can be purchased by contacting DVS Home Video.

Website: http://www.access.wgbh.org

Mailing Address:
DVS Home Video
P.O. Box 55742
Indianapolis, IN 46205

Telephone: 1-317-579-0439

To request a DVS catalog in Braille format call 1-888-818-1181.

To request a DVS catalog in large print format call 1- 888-818-1999.

To hear an audio version of the catalog or to acquire information concerning DVS call 1-800-333-1203.

II. RESOURCES FOR STUDENTS WITH HEARING IMPAIRMENTS

1. Captioned Media Program

The United States Department of Education lends open-captioned films to teachers who have students with hearing impairments in their classes. The Captioned Media Program has a catalog of over 4,000 programs that teachers can borrow. These open-captioned programs enable teachers to show captioned programming using any video cassette recorder (VCR) or DVD player. No special decoder or features are needed to show the captions.

Website: http://www.cfv.org

Mailing Address:
Captioned Media Program
National Association of the Deaf
1447 East Main Street
Spartanburg, SC 29302

Telephone (voice): 800-237-6213

Telephone (TTY): 800-237-6819

Fax: 800-538-5636

F. Directory of Websites for Elementary Teachers

The Internet can bring lesson plans, classroom management techniques, and professional development opportunities into every classroom. The websites in this directory offer advice and resources as well as an outlet for teachers to share their hopes, fears, and creativity.

This directory is divided into four sections:

I. Multi-Subject Websites

II. Single Subject Area Websites

III. Websites for Teachers of English Language Learners (ELL)

IV. Websites for Teachers of Students with Special Needs

I. MULTI-SUBJECT WEBSITES

1. A to Z Teacher Stuff

This website provides many resources and enables teachers to share ideas and seek advice from fellow educators. A special section of the website deals with the concerns of student teachers such as the interview process and classroom management.
Website: http://atozteacherstuff.com

2. AOL@School

The AOL@School website offers brainteasers, study kits, research and reference materials, and current events written for students at every grade level.
Website: http://school.aol.com/

3. Discovery School's Puzzlemaker

Puzzlemaker enables teachers and students to use their own vocabulary lists to create various types of puzzles such as cryptograms and word searches.
Website: http://www.puzzlemaker.com

You will find an electronic version of this material on the CD.

4. Education World

The Education World website has lesson plans, information on special education, and research relevant to teachers of kindergarten to grade 12.
Website: http://www.education-world.com

5. FunBrain.com

When teachers visit FunBrain.com and click on the teachers' section, they find lesson plans for every subject area and grade level activities based on the McREL standards.
Website: http://funbrain.com

6. Kathy Schrock's Guide for Educators

Like a big sister's friendly advice, Kathy Schrock's website contains the practical information and links that teachers need. With lesson plans, bulletin board ideas, rubrics, and additional resources, this site is beneficial for every educator.
Website: http://school.discovery.com/schrockguide/

7. MarcoPolo—Internet Content for the Classroom

This website, sponsored by the MarcoPolo Education Foundation, offers standards-based lesson plans that help teachers use technology in all facets of instruction.
Website: http://www.marcopolo-education.org/

8. PBS Kids

The PBS Kids website offers links to many of the children's programs that appear on Public Broadcasting Service (PBS) stations. There are games, stories, and coloring pages for children as well as background information and lesson plans for teachers.
Website: http://pbskids.org

9. PBS Teacher Source

At the PBS Teacher Source website, teachers will find lesson plans and background information for many of the programs shown on Public Broadcasting Service stations. Teachers can also register to receive a weekly e-mail newsletter alerting them to educational programming on PBS stations.
Website: http://www.pbs.org/teachersource/

II. SINGLE SUBJECT AREA WEBSITES

1. Art, Music, and the Performing Arts

American Masters Database. This website houses a database with information on over 100 talented Americans in the fields of visual arts, performing arts, music, literature, and film and television. In addition to biographical information, educators can also find related lesson plans by clicking on the teachers' section of this website.
Website: http://www.pbs.org/wnet/americanmasters/database/database_visual_arts.html

2. Health and Physical Education

American Alliance for Health, Physical Education, Recreation & Dance. The American Alliance for Health, Physical Education, Recreation & Dance website offers information on grant opportunities, professional development, and legislation affecting instruction in these areas.
Website: http://www.aahperd.org

President's Council on Physical Fitness and Sports. The President's Council on Physical Fitness and Sports website gives information on this government-sponsored program and also offers links to additional health and fitness organizations. Teachers who access this site can find suggestions for involving their students in healthy lifestyle activities.
Website: http://www.fitness.gov/

3. Mathematics

National Council of Teachers of Mathematics. The website maintained by the National Council of Teachers of Mathematics offers lesson plans and activities for students as well as information on conferences and grants for teachers.
Website: http://www.nctm.org

FunBrain.com. While this site has activities for many subject areas, there is an emphasis on mathematics with lesson plans and games for every grade level.
Website: http://funbrain.com

4. Reading and Language Arts

International Reading Association. The International Reading Association website is the teacher's link to the most current and reliable information on

literacy education. This website offers breaking news, definitions, lesson plans, and information on professional development opportunities.
Website: http://www.reading.org

Link to Literacy. Link to Literacy is a comprehensive website that provides information on word study, comprehension, the writing process, emergent literacy, children's literature, visual literacy, standards, assessment, literacy and technology, and fluency. There are lesson plans, web links, case studies, and message boards on which teachers can discuss these topics with a national audience.
Website: http://wps.prenhall.com/chet_literacy_cluster_1/0,8776,1164686-main,00.html

National Council of Teachers of English. The National Council of Teachers of English (NCTE) supports classroom teachers by offering lesson plans, grant opportunities, and news related to education on their website.
Website: http://www.ncte.org/elem

Read Write Think. Read Write Think, a website sponsored by the International Reading Association (IRA), the National Council of Teachers of English (NCTE), and the MarcoPolo Education Foundation, offers standards-based lesson plans, interactive student resources, and a directory of websites for teachers. Every Read Write Think lesson plan uses technology as an integral part of instruction.
Website: http://www.readwritethink.org

5. Science

Discovery School. The Discovery School website offers a curriculum center with activities, worksheets, puzzles, quizzes, clip art, and lesson plans to enrich instruction at every grade level.
Website: http://school.discovery.com/

NASA Explores. NASA Explores offers free weekly lesson plans and articles related to NASA projects. The lesson plans are based on the standards proposed by the National Science Teachers Association (NSTA), the National Council of Teachers of Mathematics (NCTM), the International Society for Technology in Education (ISTE), the International Technology Education Association (ITEA), and the National Geographic Society (NGS).
Website: http://www.nasaexplores.com

6. Social Studies

CNN Student News. The CNN Student News website offers news summaries, teaching tips, and articles related to education.
Website: http://cnnstudentnews.cnn.com

C-SPAN in the Classroom. C-SPAN, a private nonprofit company, began in 1979 as a public service to help citizens observe and participate in the political process. The C-SPAN in the Classroom website has video clips, grant opportunities, contests, and teaching resources that can be used to build students' understanding of government.

Website: http://www.CSPAN.org/classroom/index.asp?code=Classroom

III. WEBSITES FOR TEACHERS OF ENGLISH LANGUAGE LEARNERS (ELL)

1. National Association for Bilingual Education

The National Association for Bilingual Education represents English Language Learners and bilingual education professionals. Their website provides research and resources to help students reach their potential.

Website: http://www.nabe.org

2. Teachers of English to Speakers of Other Languages (TESOL)

With teaching resources and articles for all grade levels, the Teachers of English to Speakers of Other Languages website helps teachers provide effective English language instruction. The site contains classroom resources as well as information on conferences and other professional development opportunities.

Website: http://www.tesol.org/

IV. WEBSITES FOR TEACHERS OF STUDENTS WITH SPECIAL NEEDS

1. LD Online

LD Online provides information for teachers and families of students with learning disabilities.

Website: http://www.ldonline.org/

2. Media Access Group at WGBH

The Media Access Group at WGBH, the public television station in Boston, has engaged in many projects to make websites, television, and film accessible to individuals with disabilities. Their website contains information on educational uses of accessible programming.

Website: http://main.wgbh.org/wgbh/pages/mag/

3. National Dissemination Center for Children with Disabilities

The website of the National Dissemination Center for Children with Disabilities offers information on effective educational practices as well as summaries and guidelines on legislation such as the Individuals with Disabilities Education Act (IDEA) and No Child Left Behind (NCLB).

Website: http://www.nichcy.org

INDEX

Activities for substitute teaching, 104-105
American Alliance for Health, Physical Education, Recreation & Dance website, 155
American Association for Health, Physical Education, Recreation & Dance, 127-128, 139-140
American Association for Health Education, 121
American Council on the Teaching of Foreign Language (ACTFL), 121
American Masters Database website, 155
American Music Teacher Magazine, 140
American Printing House for the Blind, 150
AOL@School website, 153
Arrival procedures, establishing routines for, 39
Art Education: The Journal of the National Art Education Association, 139
Arts, standards for, 120
Art teachers
 journal for, 139
 professional organization for, 127
 websites for, 155
Artwork, hanging safely, 21
Assessment
 rubrics for, 89-91
 for teacher certification, 100-101
 writing samples for, 87-89
Association for Supervision and Curriculum Development (ASCD), 124
A to Z Teacher Stuff website, 153
Attendance taking, establishing routines for, 39
Audiobooks, 84

Behavior
 causes of, 45-46
 observing, 46-48
Benchmarks, 53-54

Bible reading in classroom, 114-115
Biography, sharing with students, 32
Book clubs for teachers, 108-113
 Choices lists for, 112-113
 organizing, 108
 titles for, 109-112
Bookmarks, as reward, 43
Bookshelves, securing to wall, 21
Book store displays, as source of free materials for teachers, 143
Box Tops for Education program, 144-145

Campbell's Labels for Education program, 144
Captioned Media Program (CMP), 146-147, 152
Captioned programming, 82-83
Center for Civic Education, 120
Certification, 99-101
 maintaining, 101
 NBPTS, 101
 PRAXIS Series assessments for, 100-101
Chairs, for students, comfort of, 21
Chalk, for substitute teaching, 103
Chalkboards, classroom organization and, 20
Circulation, maintaining order and, 38
Civics, standards for, 120
Classroom, inviting parents/guardians to visit, 14-15
Classroom diaries, 60
Classroom Leadership, 131
Classroom management, 37-49
 causes of behavior and, 45-46
 establishing routines for, 39-42
 maintaining order and, 38
 maintaining positive atmosphere and, 37-39
 observing behavior and, 46-48
 positive communication with parents/guardians and, 48, 49
 rewards and consequences and, 42-44
 rules for, 44-45

Classroom organization
 looking for problems with, 22, 23
 school policies regarding, 19-20
Cleaning products
 storage of, 21
 using and storing safely, 23-24
CNN Student News website, 156
Collecting homework, 66, 77
College, sharing facts about, 33-35
Community, learning about, 8-13, 15
Computer time, as reward, 43
Confidential materials, storage of, 20
Consequences, inappropriate, 44
Consistency, 39
Corporal punishment, 44
Corporate benefactors, learning about, 11-12
Corporate-sponsored programs for education, 144-146
Council for Exceptional Children (CEC), 126
Creative Classroom, 134
C-SPAN in the Classroom website, 157
Curriculum, 53
 standards versus, 54

Daily routines, 60
Decorations, school policies regarding, 19-20
Described programming, 83-84
Descriptive Video Service, 151-152
Desks, for students, comfort of, 21
Developing Educational Standards, 119
Didax Educational Resources, 119
Directions, clarity of, 39
Discovery School website, 156
Dismissal information, in substitute teacher's resource folder, 7
Dismissal procedures, establishing, 40
Displaying student work
 hanging artwork safely and, 21
 importance of, 38
Diverse classrooms
 avoiding singling out students with special needs in, 82
 IEPs and, 80-81

159

Diverse classrooms (Cont.)
  inclusion goals and, 1, 2
  media access in, 82-84
  resources for, 149-152
  role call in, 81
  seat choice in, 22, 82
Dry erase markers, for substitute teaching, 103
DVD player, location of, 21

Early childhood educators
  journals and periodicals for, 133-134
  professional organization for, 126-127
Early Childhood Research Quarterly, 134
Educational publishing, 114
Education for All Handicapped Children Act (Public Law 94-142), 79
Education Week, 132
Education World, 119
  website of, 154
Electrical outlets, classroom organization and, 21
Elementary teachers
  journals and periodicals for, 134-135
  websites for, 153-158
English Journal, 139
English language learners
  journals and periodicals for teachers of, 137
  professional organization for teachers of, 125-126
  standards for, 120
  websites for teachers of, 157
Envelopes, as source of free materials for teachers, 144
Essential Teacher, 137
Exceptional Children, 136

Faculty, working with, 6, 7
Families. *See* Parents/guardians
Field testing opportunities, 114
First day of school, 3-4
  getting to know students and, 28-32
  goal setting for, 27-28
  student teachers' introducing selves to students and, 32-35
Foreign language education, standards for, 121
Forgiveness, 49-50

Free materials for teachers, 143-148
  from corporate-sponsored programs, 144-146
  from government-sponsored programs, 146-148
  local sources of, 143-144
FunBrain.com, 154, 155
Funding Factory, 144

General education teachers
  journals and periodicals for, 131-133
  professional organizations for, 124-125
General Mills Box Tops for Education program, 144-145
Get to Know You Survey, 30-31
Goal setting, 1-2
  for first day of school, 27-28
Government education, standards for, 120
Government-sponsored programs for education, 146-148
Greeting cards, as source of free materials for teachers, 144
Greeting students and their families, 8, 10-16
Guardians. *See* Parents/guardians

Hall passes, establishing routines for, 41, 42
Health education, standards for, 121
Health teachers
  journals and periodicals for, 139-140
  professional organization for, 127-128
  websites for, 155
Hearing impairments
  captioned programming for, 82-83
  resources for, 152
  seating needs and, 22
Homework, 63-66
  collecting, 66, 77
  establishing routines for collecting, 40
  folders for, 64
  reminders for teacher about, 66
  schedule for, 64-65

Inclusion goals, 1, 2
Inclusive classrooms. *See* Diverse classrooms
Individualized Education Programs (IEPs), 80-81

Individuals with Disabilities Education Act (IDEA), IEPs and, 80-81
Instructional time, protecting, 59
Instructor, 134
Interest surveys
  for parents/guardians, 13-15
  for students, 11-12
International Reading Association (IRA), 53, 128-129
  Read Write Think website sponsored by, 156
  website of, 155-156
International Reading Association/ National Council of Teachers of English (NCTE/IRA) Standards, 122
Interstate New Teacher Assessment and Support Consortium Standards (INTASC), 118

Journal for Research in Mathematics Education (JRME), 141
The Journal of Adolescent and Adult Literacy, 138
Journal of Physical Education, Recreation, & Dance, 140

Kappa Delta Pi, 125
Kathy Schrock's Guide for Teachers website, 154

Labels for Education program, 144
Language, influence on students, 16-17, 35-36, 38
Language Arts, 138
Language arts, standards for, 122
Language arts teachers
  journals and periodicals for, 137-139
  professional organization for, 128-129
  websites for, 155-156
LD Online website, 157
Learning disabilities, audiobooks for, 84
Learning Disabilities Quarterly, 136
Learning environment
  safe and effective, creating, 19-22, 23
  using and storing materials safely and, 22-24
Lesson plans, 57-58, 66-71
  adaptive, 81
  sample, 69-71
  writing measurable objectives for, 67-68

Letters
    to explain standards to parents/guardians, 56, 57
    with interest survey for parents/guardians, 13–15
    with interest survey for students, 11–12
    to introduce student teacher to parents/guardians, 10
    requesting supplies, 16
Library access, learning about, 10
Library Reproduction Service, 150
Lineup, establishing routines for, 40–41
Link to Literacy website, 156
Literacy goals, 1, 2

The Mailbox, 135
MarcoPolo—Internet Content for the Classroom website, 154
Materials
    confidential, storage of, 20
    free. *See* Free materials for teachers
    using and storing safely, 22–24
Mathematics, standards for, 121
Mathematics Teacher (MT), 141
Mathematics teachers
    journals and periodicals for, 140–141
    professional organization for, 128
    websites for, 155
Mathematics Teaching in the Middle School (MTMS), 140
Measurable objectives, 67–68
Media access, in diverse classrooms, 82–84
Media Access Group at WGBH website, 157
Mentoring teachers, questions to ask before classes begin, 6, 7
Mid-continent Research for Education and Learning (McREL), 119–120
Middle Ground, 136
Middle Level Learning, 142
Middle School Journal, 135
Middle school teachers
    journals and periodicals for, 135–136
    professional organization for, 127
Morning messages, 60
Morning routine, establishing, 40
Movie posters, as source of free materials for teachers, 143
Music, standards for, 121

Music teachers
    journal for, 140
    professional organization for, 128
    websites for, 155
Music Teachers National Association (MTNA), 128

NASA Explores website, 156
National Art Education Association, 127
National Association for Bilingual Education website, 157
National Association for Music Education, 121
National Association for Sport and Physical Education (NASPE), 121–122
National Association for the Education of Young Children (NAEYC), 126–127
National Board for Professional Teaching Standards (NBPTS), 101, 118–118
National Braille Association (NBA), 150
National Council for Accreditation of Teacher Education (NCATE), 119
National Council for the Social Studies (NCSS), 122–123, 129–130, 141–142
National Council of Teachers of English (NCTE) website, 156
National Council of Teachers of Mathematics (NCTM), 53, 121, 128, 140–141
    website of, 155
National Dissemination Center for Children with Disabilities website, 158
National Institute for Literacy, 147
National Library Service for the Blind and Physically Handicapped, 147–148, 149–150
National Middle School Students Association, 127
National Organization of Parents of Blind Children, Slate Pals, 151
National Science Education Standards, 122
National Science Teachers Association (NSTA), 129, 141
National Standards for Art Education, 120
National Standards for Civics and Government, 120

National Standards for Foreign Language Education, 121
National Standards for Music Education, 121
Newspaper Association of America Foundation Newspaper in Education (NIE) program, 145
Newspapers, for substitute teaching, 103
The New Teacher Advocate, 132
No Child Left Behind Act (NCLB) of 2001, 53

Objectives, 53–54
    for lesson plans, 67–68
    measurable, 67–68
Observing behavior, 46–48
Online Journal for School Mathematics (ON-Math), 141

Parents/guardians
    explaining standards to, 56, 57
    interest survey for, 13–15
    inviting to visit classroom, 14–15
    letters for greeting, 8, 10, 12–15
    positive communication with, 48, 49
    responding to requests of, 96–97
Participation, encouraging, 29–32
Partnership for Reading, 147
PBS Kids website, 154
PBS Teacher Source website, 154
Performing arts teachers, websites for, 155
Phi Delta Kappa, 125
Physical education, standards for, 121–122
Physical education teachers
    journals and periodicals for, 139–140
    professional organization for, 127–128
    websites for, 155
Pizza Hut BOOK IT! Beginners Program, 145–146
Pizza Hut BOOK IT! National Reading Incentive Program, 145
Policies, flexibility regarding, 84–85
Positive communication, with parents/guardians, 48, 49
PRAXIS Series, 100–101
Prejudices, negative effects of, 24–25
President's Council on Physical Fitness and Sports website, 155

Principals, working with, 5, 6
Principal's office, sending children to, 44
Print disabilities. *See also* Visual impairments
  resources for, 149-152
Professional development, 106-107
Professional journals and periodicals, 131-142
  for early childhood educators, 133-134
  for elementary teachers, 134-135
  for general education teachers, 131-133
  for middle school teachers, 135-136
  subject-specific, 137-142
  for teachers of English language learners, 137
  for teachers of students with special needs, 136
Professional organizations, 124-130
  for art teachers, 127
  general education, 124-125
  for health and physical education teachers, 127-128
  for mathematics teachers, 128
  for middle school teachers, 127
  for music teachers, 128
  for reading and language arts teachers, 128-129
  for science teachers, 129
  for social studies teachers, 129-130
  for teachers of English language learners, 125-126
  for teachers of students with special needs, 126
  for teachers of young children, 126-127
Proximity, maintaining order and, 38
Public Law, 94-142, 79
Puzzlemaker website, 153

Questions
  to ask mentoring teachers before classes begin, 6, 7
  to ask principal before classed begin, 5, 6
Quick remarks, effects on students, 35-36
Quiet areas, location of, 20

Read-aloud selections
  in substitute teacher's resource folder, 8
  for substitute teaching, 103-104
Reading, standards for, 122
Reading logs, 93-96
Reading Research Quarterly, 138
The Reading Teacher, 137-138
Reading teachers
  journals and periodicals for, 137-139
  professional organization for, 128-129
  websites for, 155-156
Read Write Think website, 156
Recording for the Blind & Dyslexic (RFB&D), 149
Recordkeeping, 91-92
Recreational activities, learning about, 10-11
Resource folders, for substitute teachers, 7-8, 9
Review and maintenance, 60-63
Rewards
  appropriate, 42-43
  inappropriate, 43
Role call, in diverse classrooms, 81
Routines
  daily, 60
  establishing, 39-42
  maintaining, 39
Rubrics, 89-91
Rules, establishing, 44-45

Schedules
  for homework, 64-65
  in substitute teacher's resource folder, 7
Science, standards for, 122
Science and Children, 141
Science Scope, 141
The Science Teacher, 141
Science teachers
  journals and periodicals for teachers of, 141
  professional organization for, 129
  websites for, 156
Seating, in diverse classrooms, 22, 82
Sequence, for standards-based instruction, 55-56
Skills review and maintenance, 60-63
Small-group discussions, classroom organization and, 20
Snacks, as reward, 43

Social Education, 142
Social studies, standards for, 122-123
Social Studies and the Young Learner, 142
Social studies teachers
  journals and periodicals for, 141-142
  professional organization for, 129-130
  websites for, 156-157
Speaking opportunities, for students, 60
Speaking to students, 37-38
Special education teachers, collaboration with general classroom teachers, 80
Special needs students. *See also* Diverse classrooms; Hearing impairments; Visual impairments
  avoiding singling out, 82
  IEP process for, 80-81
  journals and periodicals for teachers of, 136
  professional organization for, 126
  seating for, 22
  websites for teachers of, 157-158
Specialty area classes, depriving students of, 44
Standards, 53-57, 118-123
  benefits of instruction based on, 55
  curriculum versus, 54
  definition of, 53
  directory of, 56
  displaying in classroom, 56
  expected for student teachers and novice teachers, 118-119
  explaining to parents/guardians, 56, 57
  implementing instruction based on, 55-57
  for multiple subject areas, 119-120
  for single subject areas, 120-123
Stereotypes, negative effects of, 24-25
Storing materials, classroom organization and, 20
Strategies: A Journal for Physical & Sports Educators, 140
Student contact information form, 92
Student list, in substitute teacher's resource folder, 7
Students. *See also* Diverse classrooms; Hearing impairments; Special

needs students; Visual impairments
  getting to know, 28-32
  interest survey for, 11-12
  letters for greeting, 8, 11-12
  speaking to, 37-38
Student teachers
  introducing selves to students, 32-35
  letter introducing to parents/guardians, 10
Substitute teachers
  preparing for, 6-8
  resource folder for, 7-8, 9
Substitute teaching, 102-106
  activities for, 104-105
  preparing for, 102-104
  pros and cons of, 102-103
  summary note for regular teacher and, 106
Supplies
  letter requesting, 16
  for substitute teaching, 103-104

Teacher certification. *See* Certification
Teacher Magazine, 132
Teacher's desk, location of, 21
Teachers of English to Speakers of Other Languages (TESOL), 120, 125-126, 137
  website of, 157

Teaching Children Mathematics (TCM), 140
Teaching PreK-8, 135
Technology goals, 1, 2
Technology & Learning Magazine, 133
Television, location of, 21
TESOL Connections, 137
TESOL Quarterly, 137
T.H.E. Journal, 133
T.H.E. Journal: Technological Horizons in Education program, 146
Thematic units, 57-58, 72-76
Time with teacher, as reward, 42
Transportation, learning about, 11
Trash cans, classroom organization and, 20
Travel agencies, as source of free materials for teachers, 144
Tutoring, 113

University resources, learning about, 12

Ventilation, for classroom, 24
Visits, to classroom, inviting parents/guardians to make, 14-15

Visual impairments
  described programming for, 83-84
  National Library Service for the Blind and Physically Handicapped and, 147-148
  resources for, 149-152
  seating needs and, 22
Voice, maintaining order and, 38
Voices from the Middle, 138-139

Weekly planner, 70
Whiteboards, classroom organization and, 20
Whole-group activities, classroom organization and, 20
Word of Mouse free mouse pads, 146
Word walls, for teachers, 107
Writing samples, 87-89
  to assess students' strengths and needs, 28-29
  elementary grade collection of, 88-89
Written assignments, as consequences, 44

Young Children, 133

DATE DUE

DEMCO, INC. 38-2931